D1637653

Bookkeeping and Accounting for Beginners

2 Books in 1: The Definitive Guide to Learn How to Organize and Grow your Small Business for 2020 Step-by-Step. Quickbooks and Examples (Money-Making Machine)

Warren Piper Ruell

BOOK 1

Bookkeeping for Beginners

Learn the Essential Basics of Bookkeeping for Small Businesses with Simple and Effective Methods Step-by-Step (Comprehensive Accounting, Financial Statements, and QuickBooks)

Warren Piper Ruell

Table Of Contents

BOOK 2: ACCOUNTING FOR BEGINNERS - A SIMPLE AND UPDATED GUIDE TO LEARNING BASIC ACCOUNTING CONCEPTS AND PRINCIPLES QUICKLY AND EASILY, INCLUDING FINANCIAL STATEMENTS AND ADJUSTING ENTRIES FOR SMALL BUSINESSES

Please note the information contained within this document is for educational and entertainment purposes only. All effort has been executed to present accurate, up to date, reliable, complete information. No warranties of any kind are declared or implied. Readers acknowledge that the author is not engaging in the rendering of legal, financial, medical or professional advice. The content within this book has been derived from various sources. Please consult a licensed professional before attempting any techniques outlined in this book.

By reading this document, the reader agrees that under no circumstances is the author responsible for any losses, direct or indirect, that are incurred as a result of the use of information contained within this document, including, but not limited to, errors, omissions, or inaccuracies.

Description

This book is a complete introduction to bookkeeping and accounting principles written specifically for the independent business owner.

Entrepreneurship and small business ownership are on the rise. The gig economy has created a huge upsurge in independent contractors, freelancers, and work-form-home professionals. All of this new activity in the business world is exciting, but to really succeed at running your own business, you'll need to know more than just basics of selling quality goods and service.

Starting and operating an independent business can be one of the most exciting and rewarding efforts you ever undertake. An independent business provides you with a platform to share your expertise and knowledge and use your time profitably. But there are also challenges and obstacles to overcome.

If you're like most people, you would probably prefer to spend your time representing your business to customers and clients. After all, it's your passion, and that's why you started a business to begin with, right? Don't let the idea of bookkeeping, paying bills, and learning about accounting principles dampen your enthusiasm. Learning the basics of effective bookkeeping can help you master the fundamentals of managing your business's finances. And that can free you to spend more time doing what you really love. Bookkeeping for Beginners starts with an overview of bookkeeping basics:

- What is bookkeeping?
- Why is bookkeeping important?
- How does bookkeeping work?
- What is the difference between bookkeeping and accounting?

From there, Bookkeeping for Beginners walks readers through the most impotent aspects of effective professional bookkeeping, including:

- Double-entry vs. single-entry bookkeeping.
- How to record debits and credits.
- Cash vs. accrual accounting.
- Recording assets, liabilities, expenses, income, and equity.

- Creating a chart of accounts.
- Creating and understanding financial statements.
- Using financial journals and ledgers.

Next, Bookkeeping for Beginners walks you through two case studies show you step-by-step how to:
- Set up a single-entry cash bookkeeping system.
- Set up a double-entry accrual bookkeeping system.
- Close the books and generate financial statements.

Finally, Bookkeeping for Beginners brings it all back home by covering the latest in technology and business innovation:
- Guidance on how to run a business.
- Using QuickBooks to automate bookkeeping and accounting.
- Adapting bookkeeping methods to meet the needs of your business.

Whether you are just starting out as a business owner or looking for the extra insight to make your existing business the profitable and enjoyable venture you know it can be, Bookkeeping for Beginners will set you on the track to success!

Chapter 1: Bookkeeping Basics

What is Bookkeeping?

Figure 1: Free Image

According to the *Dictionary of Business*, bookkeeping is defined simply as "the keeping of the financial records of a business or an organization." This is a fairly straightforward definition and seems obvious, but it doesn't reveal much to anyone interested in learning about how bookkeeping for small businesses works or why it is important. So, a more detailed definition will help to introduce all the topics that will be discussed throughout this book. The basic function of any bookkeeper is to record all the financial transactions that occur throughout each business day of any business. There are two important points here.

The first point is that the function of the bookkeeper is to record financial transactions – that's it. Bookkeeping does not involve analyzing the financial data to ensure compliance with tax laws, or to conduct audits, or any other complex forms of complex methods of assessing financial data. The more complex aspects of analyzing financial records and producing financial statements is the job of the accountant. Although this book will touch on some of those aspects, its main focus will be on the responsibilities of the bookkeeper. Bookkeeping is quite simply the job of ensuring that all the money that flows into and out of a business's financial accounts is recorded accurately and according to an established and organized system.

The second point is that because the primary focus of bookkeeping is ensuring that all financial transactions are recorded accurately, effective bookkeeping requires at least a basic understanding of established bookkeeping methods and which system is best for any given business. Bookkeeping systems may use one of two types of "entry systems" – single-entry and double-entry. They may also use one of two types of accounting methods – cash-based or accrual-based. We will examine the difference in greater detail later, but for now, suffice it to say that single-entry systems are best for very small businesses, while double-entry systems are more suitable for larger businesses.

Why Is Bookkeeping Important?

In this age of digital computing and the internet, many people have made the assumption that bookkeeping is obsolete. After all, the term "bookkeeping" is derived from the practice of writing down financial transactions by hand into paper ledgers or books with pages specifically designed to keep track of these types of records.

Now that the internet has spawned online banking, e-payment apps, and digital currency, many people have mistakenly assumed that these concerns are no longer relevant. But assuming that you can arrive at an accurate assessment of your business's financial condition by simply checking the balances in your business checking account online is a huge mistake. Although it is true that you can depend on the bank to maintain accurate records of deposits, withdrawals, and current balances in your bank accounts, these records are not the same as the daily transaction records of your business. The proliferation of spreadsheet software like Excel, as well as small business bookkeeping software like QuickBooks, is definitely an exciting development for all small business owners and entrepreneurs. These tools can open up the door to faster growth, greater productivity, and a more efficient and enjoyable business operation. But these tools do not replace the fundamental requirement of all businesses to maintain accurate records of their financial transactions. Effective bookkeeping can help entrepreneurs and business owners in a variety of ways, regardless of the type or size of the business they are running. Here are some of the ways your business can benefit from an effective system of bookkeeping:

- Bookkeeping ensures your personal finances will be kept separate from your business finances.

- Bookkeeping allows you to detect and correct banking, billing, and accounting errors.
- Bookkeeping allows you to optimize your business for maximum efficiency and profitability.
- Bookkeeping helps you understand where your business fits in with your overall plan for growth.
- Bookkeeping can help you qualify for tax deductions.
- Bookkeeping can help you establish better business credit and qualify for loans.

How Does Bookkeeping Work?

An effective system of bookkeeping must consider several necessary functions of your business' financial functions. Traditionally, these concerns could be addressed universally by using any standardized ledger that allowed for tracking all the daily expenses involved in running your business, as well as all of the income resulting from successful transactions.

As technology has evolved, so have bookkeeping methods. There are many bookkeeping software programs available as online services run by bookkeeping companies, as well as programs and spreadsheets that can be downloaded to your computer to allow you to complete the basic data entry and transaction recording necessary to keep your company's finances straight.

Although much of the software may make it easier to manage many of the tasks involved in bookkeeping, bookkeeping itself still requires accuracy, diligence, and attention to detail. As the computer programming slogan says, "Garbage in, garbage out." So it is with bookkeeping. Finding the right system for your business – whether you choose a more traditional paper-based system, an entirely electronic system, or some combination of both – you will need to track all the transactions that occur within your business every day. The more effective your system of bookkeeping, the easier it will be for you to check for errors, ensure consistency and accuracy, and ultimately increase profitability and accountability.

Basic Accounting Principles

As we discussed earlier, there are two major types of entry systems: single-entry accounting and double-entry accounting.

With single-entry accounting systems, all transactions – whether for financial resources that are coming into the business, or for financial resources that are flowing out of the business – are entered only once. Thus, when you receive payment for a sale, you record the transaction once as income; when you write a check to pay a bill, you record the transaction once, as an expense.

With a double entry-system, every transaction is recorded twice. In the example above, when you receive a payment for sale, you record the income as a credit, but you also debt your inventory for an equal value – the cost of the item or service you provided. In the second example, when you pay write a check to pay a bill, you may debt the business checking account for the amount of the expense, but you will also credit your monthly expense account for the same amount. Double-entry systems are more complex but also more reliable and flexible and can accommodate more growth over time.

There are also two basic accounting methods, and every bookkeeping system will use either one or the other. The two systems are cash-based accounting and accrual-based accounting.

With cash-based accounting, transactions are only recorded when the transactions actually occur. Thus, if you have bills to pay before the end of the month, you will not include them as expenses in a cash-based system until the money actually leaves the business checking account. Similarly, if you have made ten sales, you cannot count them as income until you actually receive payment from your customers.

With accrual-based accounting, you may record bills and invoices as liabilities and assets, whether or not you have paid the bills or received payment for the sales. In this system, bills that still have to be paid are called "accounts payable," and invoices that have not yet been paid are called "accounts receivable." The accrual-based system allows you to create reports that indicate projected income and projected expenses, as well as actual income and actual expenses.

Introduction to Bookkeeping and Accounting

Many people use the terms "bookkeeping" and "accounting" interchangeably. Although these two practices are related, there are several fundamental differences between them. Essentially, the difference is that the bookkeeper is responsible for recording every single transaction conducted by a business and classifying according to whether it is an expense or a form of income, as well as what type of expense and what type of income. The accountant is responsible for taking all the information about transactions compiled by the bookkeeper, analyzing that information to prepare office financial reports and statements, and making recommendations based on interpretations of the company's financial condition.

In one sense, the account's focus is narrower than that of the bookkeeper. In addition, although bookkeepers may obtain certification as a professional, their expertise is likely to come from on-the-job training and experience. Accountants, on the other hand, generally must obtain a degree in accounting and be licensed as Certified Public Accountants before they can work in any professional environment. In the hierarchy of the corporate structure, the accountant ranks higher than the bookkeeper. Although the bookkeeper may have broader knowledge and experience of bookkeeping systems, the accountant's specialized training qualifies him for more technical and complex assignments.

The following is a list of responsibilities commonly assigned to bookkeepers:

- issuing invoices to customers for goods and services sold
- receiving and documenting incoming invoices from suppliers for inventory and supplies purchased
- documenting cash, credit, and other forms of payment received from customers
- issuing payments to suppliers
- documenting changes in inventory levels
- managing payroll records
- receding and documenting petty cash transactions

By contrast, an accountant may be responsible for any of the following responsibilities:

- creating a chart of all accounts
- setting up the general ledger that will be used by the bookkeeper
- designing financial statements
- creating customized financial reports
- adjusting transaction records to ensure compliance with accounting standards
- creating budgets and comparing actual performance to benchmarks
- preparing and filing tax returns based on bookkeeping records
- creating a system of accountability
- designing record-keeping systems

Chapter 2: Bookkeeping

Principles and Fundamental

Differences

Figure 2: Free Image

If you're like most people, you probably think of the words "debit" and "credit" in terms of the kind of card you use to pay for items when you go shopping. When you use your debit card, the money comes directly out of your checking account; but when you use your credit card, instead of money being deducted from your bank account, the amount of the purchase is added to the total bill you will pay your credit card company at the end of the month.

This is a very basic understanding of debits and credits can help you navigate the terminology of this part of recording financial transactions for your business. However, in the world of bookkeeping, this essential concept is somewhat more complex.

First, before we explore the specifics of how debits and credits are used to record transactions in bookkeeping, let's consider the basic equation upon which all accounting is based:

$$Assets = Liabilities + Equity$$

Whenever you see a mathematical equation, you know that the two elements on either side of the equals sign must have the same numeric value, so the following two equations are correct:

$$2 + 1 + 1 = 4$$
$$3 + 1 = 4$$

But this equation is incorrect:

$$2 + 3 = 4$$

Because the value of a business is calculated using the accounting equation, Assets = Liabilities + Equity, the numeric values of these terms must be a balanced equation. If they are not, then your business's books are out of balance, and in order to create accurate financial statements, you will have to locate where you have made bookkeeping errors.

Next, before we examine debits and credits in detail, we should take a moment to understand the terms in the accounting equation.

- Assets are any resources that your company owns that represent a future value and can be expressed in monetary value. Cash is one type of asset, but there are many others. For example, investments, inventory, real estate, office supplies, equipment, and accounts receivable, all represent resources that you own and that can be assigned a monetary value. In addition, so-called "intangible assets" include your company's reputation, your client base, the perceived value of your brand, etc.

- Liabilities are the amount of outstanding financial obligations owed by your company. So, your company's liabilities may include the remaining balance on any mortgages, equipment leases, or business loans; accounts payable; or amounts received for future sales that have not yet been delivered.

- Equity is the amount of financial interest all of a company's shareholders have in the company. For example, if you buy 1,000 shares of stock in a new startup company at $2.25 per share, you can personally claim $2,250.00 of that company's value as yours.

So, the accounting equation, Assets = Liabilities + Equity, means that in order for your company's books to be considered balanced and in order, you must be able to show that the total value of all of your assets is exactly equal to the total value of all your liabilities plus the total value of all of the equity all shareholders may have in your company. This seems like a daunting task, and that's why accounting uses both debits and credits to record transactions.

Importance of Debit and Credit Accounting

We began this chapter by considering a common understanding of debits and credits – using your debit card takes money out of your checking account; using a credit card adds money to your credit card bill. This is a great start to understanding the importance of using debits and credits to keep accurate books, but in terms of bookkeeping, this concept is more complex.

First, consider the definition of assets above. There are many types of assets, ranging from the balance in your business's main checking account, to the total value of your inventory, to the value of your supplies and equipment, to the value of all the sales you have made for which you are awaiting payment. As a result, an accurate bookkeeping system will need more than just one account to track assets.

Next, you may also have many types of liabilities, including accounts payable and future sales, so you may have more than one account to record all your liabilities.

Finally, in addition to assets, liabilities, and equity, your bookkeeping system will have to keep track of revenue, expenses, gains, and losses.

Taken together, these categories of financial accounts – assets, liabilities, equity, revenue, expenses, gains, and losses – comprise what accountants call the chart of accounts and depending on the size and complexity of your company, the chart of accounts can become fairly complicated.

One more step, and the importance of debits and credits will become clear. Returning to the original example of shopping at your local department store, consider what happens when you buy something with your debit card – the amount of money in your checking account is reduced, but the amount of money in the department store's checking account is increased. In addition, although you have less cash after making the purchase with the debit card, you have increased the value of your assets by the value of the term you purchased; and in return, the value of the store's inventory has decreased by the value of the time they sold. The difference in making the purchase with a credit card is that instead of decreasing the amount of money in your checking account, you increase the amount of money you owe; similarly, the store does not receive an increase in the amount of money in their checking account, but they do see an increase in the value of their accounts receivable.

Thus, the concept behind debits and credits is that every single transaction has two parts – money is taken from one account, and money is added to another account. Because a company's books account for a potentially complex chart of accounts, a system of debits and credits allows the bookkeeper to record all transactions accurately and consistently.

Recording Debit and Credit in an Account

Figure 3: Free Image

First, remember that in accounting, debit is abbreviated dr. and credit is abbreviated cr. Second, although it is common to associate debit with deducting money and credit with adding money, debits and credits in bookkeeping are used differently. Depending on which type of transaction the company engages in and which type of account is affected, debits and credits may either increase or decrease the value of any given account. Specifically:

- For asset accounts (e.g., your company's checking account):
  - A debit will increase the value of the account; a credit will decrease the value of the account.
- For liability accounts (e.g., your accounts payable account):
  - A debit will decrease the value of the account; a credit will increase the value of the account.
- For equity accounts (e.g., the shares an investor holds in your company):
  - A debit will decrease the value of the account; a credit will increase the value of the account.

This seems to be the reverse order of the way you may normally think of debits and credits because it is based on the accounting equation, Assets = Liabilities + Equity. Thus, you cannot increase your assets unless you also increase your liabilities or equity. As a result, debits and credits within a bookkeeping system function differently than in a simple check register.

Of course, in some cases, recording a balanced transaction may require increasing the value of one asset account while decreasing the value of another asset account (instead of a liability or equity account). In these cases, there are additional rules that govern the function of debits and credits:

- For revenue accounts:
    - A debit decreases the balance and a credit increases the balance.
- For expense accounts:
    - A debit will increase the balance and a credit will decrease the balance.
- For gain accounts:
    - A debit decreases the balance and a credit increases the balance.
- For loss accounts:
    - A debit will increase the balance and a credit will decrease the balance.

Regardless, in terms of an actual book of accounts, debits are transaction values that are entered on the left side of an account, and credits are transaction values that are entered on the right side of an account.

Third, for every single transaction in bookkeeping, the total amount recorded as a debit must be offset by the exact same amount recorded as credit. If the two sides of the transaction are unequal, the books will not balance, and the bookkeeping system will not accept the entry.

Let's look at some specific examples to clarify the concepts above.

For the first example, let's assume your company sells computer accessories. One of your customers purchases a video camera attachment for a laptop computer at a cost of $375.00. The sale results in an increase in the value of your cash account. It also means that you have increased your revenue by converting inventory into cash. To record this transaction using debits and credits, the bookkeeper will use two accounts: cash and revenue. When you sold the camera attachment to the customer, you received $375.00 in cash, so the cash account is debited for 375. To record the associated increase in revenue, the bookkeeper credits the revenue account for the same amount – 375.

Account	Debit	Credit
Cash	375	
Revenue		375

Alternatively, the records may be displayed as follows:

Cash	
Debits	Credits
375	

Revenue	
Debits	Credits
	375

In the next example, let's assume that your company needs 10 new servers, and each server costs $1,000. You don't want to use your cash account to make this purchase, so you instruct your purchasing agent to buy them on credit. The purchase results in an increase to the value of your fixed assets account. Because they were purchased on credit, there will be an equal increase to the value of your accounts payable. Here is how the bookkeeper will record the transaction:

Account	Debit	Credit
Fixed Assets	10,000	
Accounts Payable		10,000

Again, the same relationship can be displayed as follows:

Fixed Assets	
Debits	Credits
375	

Accounts Payable

Debits	Credits
	375

Finally, here are some additional guidelines to help get you oriented to the world of debits and credits:

1. Debit-Credit Table

Account Type	Increase	Decrease
Assets	Debit	Credit
Expenses	Debit	Credit
Liabilities	Credit	Debit
Equity	Credit	Debit
Revenue	Credit	Debit

2. Debit-Credit Acronyms

The following types of accounts (DEAL) are increased with a debit:

- Dividends
- Expenses
- Assets

- <u>L</u>osses

The following types of accounts (GIRLS) are increased with a credit:

- <u>G</u>ains
- <u>I</u>ncome
- <u>R</u>evenues
- <u>L</u>iabilities
- <u>S</u>tockholders' Equity

3. Debit-Credit Rules

Recording a debit means:

- Increasing the value of an asset account
- Increasing the value of an expense account
- Decreasing the value of a liability account
- Decreasing the value of an equity account
- Decreasing the value of revenue
- Debits are always recorded on the left

Recording a credit means:

- Decreasing the value of an asset account
- Decreasing the value of an expense account
- Increasing the value of a liability account
- Increasing the value of an equity account

- Increasing the value of revenue
- Credit are always recorded on the right

The Accrual Method of Bookkeeping

Now that you have a basic understanding of debits and credits and how they are used to record transactions, we will discuss the accrual method of bookkeeping. When a bookkeeper uses accrual-based accounting, he or she will record all transactions based on when the transaction occurs, rather than when money changes hands. For example, if you make a sale in January, but you don't expect the invoice to be paid until March, a bookkeeper using the accrual method will record the sale in January rather than waiting until the invoice is paid. Similarly, if you sell goods or services to a client on credit, the accrual method of bookkeeping allows you to claim the entire sale at the time the transaction takes place, rather than recording partial sale every time an installment payment is received. Accounting for purchases and expenses using the accrual method is similar – for purchases made on credit, the entire expense, not just the amount of money that changes hands – is recorded at the time of the transaction.

Differences between the Accrual Method and the Cash Method

The cash-based method of bookkeeping is based on cash flow rather than credit and accounts receivable. When a bookkeeper uses the cash-based method, he will only record transactions when cash is paid or received. Thus, if you make a sale, deliver the goods, and send an invoice to your customer in January, but your customer does not send you a check until March, the bookkeeper will record the sale in March, when the payment is received, not in January, when the sale was made. Similarly, if you incur expenses to deliver goods or services to a customer, a bookkeeper using a cash-based method will record the expenses at the time you pay for them, rather than making them part of the entire cost of the sale in the invoice to the customer. For example, if you have to travel to another town to access confidential files as part of generating a professional report, the accrual-based method would allow the bookkeeper to defer recording the cost of those expenses until the invoice is generated; using the cash-based method, the daily expenses of any contract will be recorded as they are incurred and paid by the employee.

The essential difference between these two methods is that the accrual-based method can allow your bookkeeper to create a more accurate picture of your overall income and expenses; as a result, it is a better method for business owners concerned about monitoring their profitability. On the other hand, the strength of the cash-based method of bookkeeping is that you will have a better picture of your daily cash flow.

You will have to identify which type of bookkeeping method you use when you file your taxes, and if you change the method, you will have to notify the Internal Revenue Service by filing a Form 3115, Change in Accounting Method. In addition, if you use an accrual-based method of accounting, you have to use the double-entry method of bookkeeping. We examined the double-entry method, which uses debits and credits, above. The next two sections discuss the differences between double-entry accounting and single-entry accounting.

Single-Entry Bookkeeping (Advantages and Disadvantages)

Single-entry bookkeeping can be compared to keeping track of transaction in your check register. Bookkeeping methods that use the single-entry method only require the bookkeeper to record transactions as they are made, usually bills that are paid from or deposits that are placed into the company's main checking account. This fairly simple form of bookkeeping is appropriate for small companies that do not engage in many transactions. The following is an example of a transaction record using the single-entry method:

Cash Account				
Date	Transaction	Debit	Credit	Balance
January 1, 2020	Balance forward			$100,000.00
January 5, 2020	Payment received	$2,500.00		$102,500.00
January 7, 2020	Rent paid		$750.00	$101,750.00

January 10, 2020	Payroll processed		$40,000.00	$61,750.00
January 12, 2020	Cash sale	$8,000.00		$69,750.00
January 15, 2020	Payment received	$5,500.00		$75,250.00
January 17, 2020	Equipment purchased		$2,000.00	$73,250.00
January 20, 2020	Cash sale	$5,000.00		$78,250.00
January 25, 2020	Utilities paid		$450.00	$77,800.00
January 30, 2020	Payment received	$2,000.00		$79,800.00

Clearly, the advantage with single-entry bookkeeping is the simplicity of the system. A short learning curve and the immediate accessibility and transferability of this kind of bookkeeping from your experiences in personal finance to business bookkeeping makes it an attractive option.

However, if your business has any degree of complexity, or if you require a more accurate method of tracking your expenses, single-entry bookkeeping may not address your needs.

Double-Entry Method (Advantages and Disadvantages)

We discussed the double-entry method in the section above entitled, "Recording Debit and Credit in an Account." This type of accounting is obviously more complex that single-entry bookkeeping, However, as we have discussed, only the double-entry method will allow you to record complex transactions that involve more than one type of account. In addition, double-entry accounting can allow you to create a more accurate picture of your company's overall financial condition, including current profitability and cost efficiency. These models can be used to generate reports and make predictions for future growth, secure funding, and identify opportunities for tax breaks or optimization.

Differences Between Excel and Other Software

The system of debits and credits that is used throughout all accounting systems in the contemporary global environment was developed by a Franciscan monk long before even the electric calculator was invented, let alone the mainframe computer, the digital phone, or virtual bookkeeping spreadsheets, apps, and services.

Traditionally, even the most complex accounting and bookkeeping systems were all maintained by entering transactions by hand into paper ledgers. Some argue that the discipline required to maintain paper ledgers and account journals translates into greater fiscal awareness and better business development and policy making decisions. There is much truth to these sentiments; however, it is not reasonable to expect everyone to return to keeping paper-based records of the company's transactions. Regardless, it is important to consider the purpose and the nature of bookkeeping when you are deciding on the tools and methods to use to keep track of your company's finances.

Microsoft Excel spreadsheets are very versatile and can be adapted to a wide variety of uses. The section on Single-Entry Bookkeeping was created using an Excel spreadsheet. Considering that bookkeeping and accounting had existed primarily as a paper-based practice for most of time, it is possible to adapt Excel spreadsheets for any type of bookkeeping system – single-entry; double-entry; cash-based; or accrual-based. However, a more appropriate use of Excel spreadsheets is to assist the bookkeeper in maintaining accurate paper-based documents. In such cases, most bookkeepers in these cases would likely be utilizing a single-entry cash-based system.

Bookkeeping software has reached a high stage of development, so that many of the functions discussed in this chapter – balancing double-entry transactions and creating reports in accrual-based systems, for example – have been automated. However, simply because the functions themselves have been automated does not mean that the software will do the accounting for you. If you enter the debits and credits of a transaction in a double-entry system incorrectly, the software may refuse to accept the entry or otherwise alert you to the error, but it is still the bookkeeper's responsibility to ensure the accuracy of all financial information entered into the program. Garbage in; garbage out – any accounting or bookkeeping software you use is only as good as the accuracy and completeness of the transaction information you enter into it.

Chapter 3: Assets, Liabilities, and Capital

Chapter 2 discussed how a system of bookkeeping for a company with any degree of complexity will use a chart of accounts (COA) to enable the accurate double-entry of transactions using debits and credits. Chapter 2 also identified the main types of account categories these bookkeeping systems use. In this chapter, we will look at many of the different types of accounts a company may list in its COA. In the first part of this chapter, we will identify the main standardized categories of accounts. The second part of the chapter will give examples of all the many types of accounts that can be included under each of the five main account types.

Figure 4: Free Image

Account Categories

Regardless of the size of your company or the type of business services or goods you offer, all the accounts in your COA should fall under one of the five main categories of account types:

- Assets
- Expenses
- Liabilities
- Equity

- Revenue and/or Income

We will also briefly discuss a sixth possible account category:

- Contra-account

General Account Categories

Let's begin by briefly defining and describing the main accounting categories:

Assets

Anything that your company owns that has value can be considered an asset. Assets can be "tangible," i.e., actual, real property such as cash; machinery and equipment; inventory; land; and buildings. Assets can also be "intangible," i.e., things that may have value but that are not actual products or physical objects, such as trademarks; a client base; or a reputation for excellence.

Expenses

Expenses are all the costs associated with running your business. Depending on the complexity and size of your business, you may have many types of expenses. For example, a small business will have to spend money on office supplies, postage, rent, and utilities. Larger businesses will likely have these expenses, but they may also have to spend money on payroll administration, workers' compensation insurance, and travel.

Liabilities

In a sense, liabilities are the opposite of assets. Your liability accounts will list all the money your company owes. There may be many reasons your company owes money. For example, taxes on your payroll account; money you owe to other businesses for equipment purchases; and business loans at your local bank all represent fixed sums that you must pay to outside parties.

Revenue or Income

These accounts represent the amount of money your business earns from selling products or services to customers. Income accounts usually refer to money your company earns from investments, such as interest-bearing accounts with banks or other investment accounts.

Equity

All of your equity accounts represent the amount of money invested in your business or retained as revenue kept as an asset. Recall the basic accounting equation, Assets = Liabilities + Equity. Using a little basic math, we can solve this equation for Equity as follows: Assets - Liabilities = Equity. So, if you total up the value of your assets and subtract everything you owe, what's left is your Equity; this figure tells you how much your company is worth. Depending on the type of business you have, your equity accounts may range from retained earnings to common stock.

Contra-accounts

Not everyone uses contra-accounts. They are created as an accounting tool to offset discrepancies in the rest of your accounts. For example, you may have an account for bad debt allowance, so that if any of your customers fails to pay one of your accounts receivable, you will have a place to record the transaction.

Specific Account Types

Within each account category, any given company may have a wide variety of differing accounts. As you are setting up your COA, it is important to consider all of the types of assets, liabilities, expenses, revenue and equity your company currently has, and what you reasonably expect to encounter as your business grows. A bookkeeping account should be created for each of these concerns, and you will have to decide under which category each of the accounts should be placed.

To help you gain an understanding of how a COA should be structured, this section begins with examples of the many types of accounts that may be included within each of the categories above, and then provides a sample COA. Let's begin by looking at the many types of account you may place under each of the account categories.

Asset Accounts

It's easy enough to understand that assets are things that have value that your company owns. But you can't just total up everything you own, then place the amount in one huge asset account. Even your company's cash reserves will have to separate into different accounts – main checking account (cash) and petty cash, with retained earnings placed in a revenue account. The reason for this specificity is to allow for more control over your company's finances. For example, you will pay all your monthly bills and routine expenses out of your cash account, but you should also fund a petty cash account, so employees have access to funds for unexpected per diem accounts and unplanned purchases. The following is a list of some of the types of accounts commonly listed under Assets:

- Cash: There may be serval cash accounts or only one, depending on the structure of your company. If you have more than one account into which you make deposits or withdraw money for purchase, each of them should be identified:
  - Petty cash
  - Business Checking
  - Business Savings
- Accounts receivable. Total amount of all unpaid invoices sent to customers for goods and services sold. This account is separate from cash because you have not received the money yet.
- Inventory. The total value of all items your company currently possesses, and that you intend to sell.
- Equipment. The total value of all business equipment that you have purchased and own outright.
- Buildings. The total value of any buildings your company owns.
- Land. The total value of all undeveloped land your company owns.
- Investments. The total value of all securities investments your company owns.

- Prepaid expenses. If your company prepays expenses such as rent or insurance, you may create an account to keep track of the value:
  - Prepaid rent
  - Prepaid insurance
- Supplies. This may be included as part of the equipment account, or you may create a separate account, depending on the nature and complexity of your business.

Expense Accounts

As discussed above, all accounts under the Expenses category should relate to costs associated with producing goods or services, or otherwise with the day-to-day administration of your business. Because accurate bookkeeping requires that you record every single transaction, no matter how small, creating accurate expense accounts is a must. Following are some examples of the types of Expense accounts many businesses may use:

- Cost of Goods Sold (COGS): If you manufacture the goods you sell, you will incur the expenses related to purchasing the material to produce them. Alternatively, you may purchase the items at wholesale and sell them at retail; in this case, the COGS is the amount you pay for the inventory you sell.

- Supplies. If your company produces goods and services, the cost of all supplies required for those purposes should be recorded here.

- Utilities. The monthly cost of electricity, gas, water, and other utility bills should be recorded here.

- Payroll. You may have many different accounts under the payroll heading, depending on the size and complexity of your company.

- Rent. If your company rent retail or office space, you can record transactions here.

- Insurance. Depending on what type of business you operate and insurance regulations, there may be several types of insurance premiums you may have to pay. Record those transactions here.

- Equipment. If your company leases equipment, you can record payments here.

- Advertising. Any expenses associated with marketing and advertising should be recorded here.

- Fees. Increasingly, banks and other institutions may charge fees for their essential services.

These are expenses that are separate from the service you are paying for, so you should record them in a separate account.

Liability Accounts

Liabilities are different from expenses. Think of expenses as the monthly or daily costs associated with running your business. Liabilities represent a fixed amount of money that you owe to outside third parties. Generally, you assume liabilities as part of the overall investment for starting and/or growing your business. The following are some examples of the type of Liability accounts many businesses will record in their ledgers:

- Accounts payable. All outstanding financial obligations that the company has not yet paid.
- Sales tax payable. Especially if you sell goods and services online, your company may be required to keep track of the sales tax you owe and pay the IRS annually or quarterly. This account will help you record these transactions.
- Salaries payable. Prior to distributing payroll checks to your employees, the

hours they work will accumulate total amounts payable in this account.

- Retirement contributions payable. If your company provides employees with retirement accounts with matching contributions, you can record transactions here.
- Mortgage payable. If you have bought a building for your business and you still owe money on the mortgage, you should record all associated transactions here.
- Taxes payable. Your business may be responsible for a variety of tax obligations, and separate accounts can be set up for each of them:
  - Federal unemployment tax payable.
  - Federal income tax payable.
  - State unemployment tax payable.
  - State income tax payable.
  - Social security tax payable.
- Interest payable. If you have taken out any business loans, you can record amortized interest payable here.

Revenue or Income Accounts

Your business's revenue is the money you earn by providing the goods and services you produce. These accounts track the money you bring as a result of successful business transactions. Typical revenue accounts include:

- Service revenue. If your company provides services, such as accounting, legal services, photography, or plumbing, you should use this account to record each payment received from a customer every time you perform a service.
- Sales revenue. If your business primarily sells products, use this account to record the total value of all receipts for goods sold.
- Interest earned. If your company keeps cash in any interest-bearing bank or investment accounts, you can record payment here.
- Dividends earned. Similar to the interest earned account, all payments received from securities investments that pay shareholders dividends should be recorded here.

Equity Accounts

Equity accounts are used to record all transactions related to money invested in the business. This section of your COA will vary in complexity depending on the type of business you have. Examples of Equity accounts include:

- Capital. This type of equity account is used by small businesses – sole proprietorships and limited partnerships – to record the amount of money the owner has invested in the business.

- Withdrawal. Also used by sole-proprietors or limited partnerships, this type of account is used to record money taken out of the business for the personal use of the owner.

- Common Stock. Corporations use a common stock account to record the transactions of shareholders who purchase stock in the company.

- Retained Earnings. The counterpart to the Withdrawal account for smaller businesses, this account records transactions related to the payments of dividends or other earnings distributions to owners and shareholders.

Contra-accounts

All the account types above may involve transactions that involve discrepancies, or for which there may not be any specific account set up. In order to ensure your books balance, Contra-Accounts provide a method of rectifying accounting discrepancies. Some examples include:

- Accumulated depreciation. The value of your equipment in assets may decline as a result of depreciation. You can record those values here.

- Bad debt allowance. Your Accounts Receivable account lists all the money your customers owe you for goods sold or services provided. Sometimes, your customers may default on the invoice. You can record the value of unpaid invoices here.

Sample Chart of Accounts

Below is a sample of how your company's COA may be structured. Notice that a range of numbers is assigned to the accounts within each category. By allowing for larger gaps between the ranges of numbers, you will be able to accommodate any unforeseen changes or growth to your company's business structure.

ABC Goods and Services, Inc.	
Chart of Accounts	
Asset Accounts	
	100 Checking
	101 Petty Cash
	102 Savings
	105 Accounts Receivable
	110 Inventory
	111 Equipment
	125 Buildings and land

Expense Accounts

200 Cost of Goods Sold

205 Payroll

207 Utilities

210 Rent

215 insurance

220 Equipment leases

230 Fees

Liability Accounts

300 Accounts payable

301 Taxes payable

305 Salaries payable

320 Mortgage payable

330 Taxes payable

350 Interest payable

Revenue Accounts

400 Sales revenue
500 Service Revenue
600 Interest Earned
650 Dividends earned

Equity Accounts

700 Capital Invested
750 Withdrawals

Contra Accounts

800 Depreciation
900 Bad debts

Chapter 4: Financial Statements

Throughout the year, the bookkeeper will record and categorize every single transaction in which a company engages, with each transaction placed in the appropriate account. If all these bookkeeping entries are accurate, the books will balance at the end of the year. This information allows the business owner to effectively monitor his or her company's operations and look for ways to improve efficiency, save money, or make new investments. Equally important, well-kept books allow the business owner to produce financial statements that comply with Generally Accepted Accounting Principles (GAAP).

Figure 5: Free Image

What is a Financial Statement?

So, what are these financial statements, and why are they so important? Briefly, financial statements are written records of a company's business and financial activity over the course of previous year designed to convey information about the company's financial performance to shareholders, prospective investors, or regulatory agencies. Accountants prepare financial statements using the information recorded by bookkeepers. All financial statements must comply with GAAP-based formatting and content standards. In many cases, financial statements are audited by private accounting firms or government agencies prior to their release to ensure the information is accurate and reliable.

All financial statements include three major sections:

- Balance sheet
- Income statement
- Cash flow statement

The following sections discuss the uses of financial statements, as well as a detailed examination of each part of a financial statement.

Who Reads Financial Statements?

Financial statements are released to a wide variety of audiences for many different reasons. Possible recipients of financial statements may include:

- Shareholders who want to review the financial statement to evaluate their current investment in a company.

- Investors who are considering investing in a company and want to examine the company's financial performance.

- Brokers, market analysts, and financial advisers who are responsible for recommending investments to their clients.

- Creditors who have to make a decision about whether to lend money to a business.

- Financial regulators and auditors who are hired to investigate a company's financial activity.

Regardless of who is reading the financial statements, the information they convey may serve a variety of purposes, such as:

- The ability of a company to generate cash.
- The ability of a company to pay its debts.
- The overall profitability of a company wand whether it has optimized the use of its resources.
- To determine the soundness of a company's financial structure and its underlying business operations.
- To investigate any of the business's transactions to ensure there are no deviations for GAAP-based standards, legal requirements, or other regulations.

Balance Sheets

The first part of a GAAP-compliant financial statement is the balance sheet. The information included in a balance sheet is designed to provide an overview of a company's assets, liabilities, and equity. Remember again that the basic accounting equation is Assets = Liabilities + Equity. The balance sheet provides a breakdown of these three financial considerations. The main purpose of the balance sheet is to identify how assets are funded – with liabilities like debt, or with equity like capital invested or retained earnings. Generally, a balance sheet will list assets in order of liquidity and liabilities in the order in which they are expected to be paid. Many balance sheets will reflect the format of the basic accounting equation: assets will be listed on the left; liabilities and equity will be listed on the right. Alternatively, assets may be listed at the top, followed by liabilities, and then equity.

One of the most important aspects of the balance sheet to remember is that the information about the company's financial condition it conveys represents only "a snapshot in time." That is, the information about a company's assets, liabilities, and equity as conveyed in a balance sheet is true only for the period of time at which the balance sheet was prepared. So, if the end of the fiscal year is December, and the date of the balance sheet is December 31, the information contained in the balance sheet is true for December 31 of that year only. Though drastic changes are unlikely to occur in the near future, the balance sheet does not convey the company's financial condition over the entire previous year for which the report was created.

The following is an example of a balance sheet:

[Company Name]

Balance Sheet
Date:

Assets	2014	2013
Current Assets		
Cash	11,874	
Accounts receivable		
Inventory		
Prepaid expenses		
Short-term investments		
Total current assets	11,874	-
Fixed (Long-Term) Assets		
Long-term investments	1,208	
Property, plant, and equipment	15,340	
(Less accumulated depreciation)	(2,200)	
Intangible assets		
Total fixed assets	14,348	-
Other Assets		
Deferred income tax		
Other		
Total Other Assets	-	-
Total Assets	26,222	-

Liabilities and Owner's Equity		
Current Liabilities		
Accounts payable	8,060	
Short-term loans		
Income taxes payable	3,145	
Accrued salaries and wages		
Unearned revenue		
Current portion of long-term debt		
Total current liabilities	11,205	-
Long-Term Liabilities		
Long-term debt	3,450	
Deferred income tax		
Other		
Total long-term liabilities	3,450	-
Owner's Equity		
Owner's investment	7,178	
Retained earnings	4,389	
Other		
Total owner's equity	11,567	-
Total Liabilities and Owner's Equity	26,222	-

Common Financial Ratios		
Debt Ratio (Total Liabilities / Total Assets)	0.56	
Current Ratio (Current Assets / Current Liabilities)	1.06	
Working Capital (Current Assets - Current Liabilities)	669	-
Assets-to-Equity Ratio (Total Assets / Owner's Equity)	2.27	
Debt-to-Equity Ratio (Total Liabilities / Owner's Equity)	1.27	

Income Statements

The second part of a GAAP-compliant financial statement is the income statement. People often use the term "bottom line" in reference to the final cost of something or the final result of some type of analysis. This term is actually taken from the income statement, because the final assessment of how much money a company made for a given period of time will always be located on the bottom line of the income statement. Unlike balance sheets, income statements report financial activity over a period of time – usually either an entire financial year, or a financial quarter. The income statement shows all the profit and all the expenses the company earned for that period; sometimes, it may be referred to as a profit and loss statement.

The income statement includes very specific information about a company's income and expenses. For example, income is divided into operating income, non-operating income, and other income. Operating income is all the money a company earned as a result of performing its main business functions. For example, if you own a restaurant, operating income is all the money you earn from preparing and selling meals. Non-operating income is money earned through means that are not the direct result of the business's main focus. For example, the following types of income may be considered non-operating income:

- Interest earned from money deposited in bank accounts;
- Rental income from properties the business may own.

Other income is income earned from financial activity completely unrelated to the business's main function. Examples of other income include:

- Money earned from the sale of real estate, vehicles, or other fixed assets.
- Money earned from the sale of subsidiaries.

The income statement also specifies all the different types of operating expenses the company incurred. Expenses are separated into two categories, as well – primary expenses and secondary expenses. Primary expenses are all the expenses directly related to the production of goods and services sold and to the general administrative costs of running the business. Primary expenses may include:

- Cost of Goods Sold (COGS)
- Research and development
- Employee wages
- Utility and transportation bills
- Depreciation (the loss of value of machinery and equipment used to produce goods and services)

Secondary expenses are indirectly related to the main business operations and may include costs such as:

- Interest paid on loans
- Debts
- Losses associated with the sale of assets

Finally, like all GAAP-compliant financial statements, income statements must follow a predetermined format to report a company's quarterly or annual income. You can think of the income statement as a reverse pyramid, with the big, wide base at the top. At the tops of the statement, you will see the company's "gross income" or gross revenue." This is just the big, unrefined number that results from adding up all the sources of income over the quarter or year.

The next part of the statement shows the expense resulting from income the company may not collect due to sales, discounts, or other reasons. This deduction may be called the "cost of sales" and deducting it from the gross income results in the "net income" or "net revenue."

Operating expenses are detailed next. All the operating expenses are listed, with specific costs associated with each type of expense. Generally, this is where the company will list all the administrative costs of its business operations. By deducting operating expenses from gross profit, you result in a figure called, "income from operations."

Non-operating income and expenses are generally detailed next. These are usually either income or expenses resulting from interest earned or paid; investment returns; or dividends paid out. Some income statements separate interest income and expenses; other statements may combine them. The final amount of this calculation is combined with the income from operations and results in operating profit before tax.

The final step in the income statement process is deducting income tax. The amount of income tax the company paid for the quarter or year is entered here. It is deducted from the operating profit before tax, and the result is net income, net profit, or net earnings. It will be located on the bottom line of the income statement.

The following is an example of an income statement:

[Company Name]

Income Statement

For the Years Ending [Dec 31, 2016 and Dec 31, 2017]

Revenue	2017	2016
Sales revenue	110,000	95,000
(Less sales returns and allowances)		
Service revenue	70,000	62,000
Interest revenue		
Other revenue		
Total Revenues	**180,000**	**157,000**

Expenses		
Advertising	1,000	1,000
Bad debt		
Commissions		
Cost of goods sold	65,000	63,000
Depreciation		
Employee benefits		
Furniture and equipment		8,000
Insurance		
Interest expense	4,200	5,200
Maintenance and repairs		
Office supplies		
Payroll taxes		
Rent		
Research and development		
Salaries and wages	55,000	55,000
Software		
Travel		
Utilities		
Web hosting and domains		
Other	17,460	
Total Expenses	**142,660**	**132,200**
Net Income Before Taxes	37,340	24,800
Income tax expense	14,936	9,920
Income from Continuing Operations	**22,404**	**14,880**

Below-the-Line Items		
Income from discontinued operations		
Effect of accounting changes		
Extraordinary Items		
Net Income	**22,404**	**14,880**

80

Cash Flow Statements

Finally, the cash flow statement (CFS) completes the three major parts of a financial statement. As we have seen, the balance sheet provides a snapshot of a company's current assets and liabilities. The income statement provides documentation of a company's profitability. The cash flow statements complete this picture of financial activity by showing not only what a company is worth or whether it has been profitable in the previous financial period, but whether it has been able to generate cash to support its business operations. Like the income statement, the CFS shows changes over a period of time, but the CFS focuses on the net increase or decrease in available cash for a company's business operations. The CFS is divided into three sections: operating activities; investing activities; and financing activities. The net increase or decrease in available cash is shown in the bottom line of the CFS.

• Operating Activities

The operating activities section of the CFS documents all activity related to sources or uses of cash resulting from the main operating concern of the business. So, cash from operating activities may include changes to cash accounts, accounts receivable, inventory, accounts payable, wages, income tax, and other operating expenses like rent, depreciation, and interest payments. Essentially, the Operating Activities section of the CFS reconciles the net income for the Income Statement to the amount of actual cash the company has received from its business operations.

• Investing Activities

This section of the CFS documents all cash flow related to investment activity. For example, if a company purchases long-term fixed assets, such as land, buildings, plants, and equipment, the Investing Activities section of the CFS shows the outflow of cash used to make the investments. Similarly, if a company sells any of its assets or securities investments, the proceeds would be recorded in this section of the CFS.

•   Financing Activities

This section of the CFS records all changes in cash flow
resulting from activity related to financing. For example, cash
raised as a result of selling shares to stockholders or
borrowing money from banks appears in this section of the
CFS. In addition, any changes in cash flow resulting from loan
payments or other money owed for financed investments
would also show up here.

The following is an example of a Cash Flow Statement:

[Company Name]
Cash Flow Statement

For the Year Ending		12/31/15
Cash at Beginning of Year		15,700

Operations

Cash receipts from		
Customers		693,200
Other Operations		
Cash paid for		
Inventory purchases		(264,000)
General operating and administrative expenses		(112,000)
Wage expenses		(123,000)
Interest		(13,500)
Income taxes		(32,800)
Net Cash Flow from Operations		147,900

Investing Activities

Cash receipts from		
Sale of property and equipment		33,600
Collection of principal on loans		
Sale of investment securities		
Cash paid for		
Purchase of property and equipment		(75,000)
Making loans to other entities		
Purchase of investment securities		
Net Cash Flow from Investing Activities		(41,400)

Financing Activities

Cash receipts from		
Issuance of stock		
Borrowing		
Cash paid for		
Repurchase of stock (treasury stock)		
Repayment of loans		(34,000)
Dividends		(53,000)
Net Cash Flow from Financing Activities		(87,000)

Net Increase in Cash   **19,500**

Cash at End of Year		35,200

Chapter 5: Ledger for

Bookkeeping

The first four chapters of this book have outlined many of the basic principles of bookkeeping. In addition, Chapter 4 discusses financial statements, which provide a standardized and accepted method of presenting the information recorded by a bookkeeper to potential investors, shareholders, and financial regulators. Understanding these basic principles is essential to ensuring that your company's financial records are accurate and reliable. However, the initial chapters of this book have focused more on the end-result of bookkeeping rather than the day-to-day practice of recording transactions throughout a given fiscal period, so that when the end of the quarter or year arrives, your books will be balanced and ready for closing, and all the necessary information will be available for your accountant to prepare financial statements.

The remainder of this book focuses on the details of keeping and maintaining accurate financial records as part of your effort to run an efficient and profitable business venture. This chapter focuses on the two most important depositories of bookkeeping records: the financial journal and the general ledger. Traditionally, both the journal and the ledger were always bound, paper volumes with pages designed specifically to enable the accurate recording of transactions. Because these volumes were always in book form, the term "bookkeeping" was used to describe the profession of maintaining financial records.

As a result of digital technology, many companies now use computer software to record transactions. Although these software applications offer many advantages, such as the ability to search for transactions or simpler entry of information about transactions, the digital versions of these volumes of bookkeeping data have retained the same names – journals and ledgers. In fact, in most cases, even large corporations who depend on the efficiency of automated bookkeeping software have found that to some degree, recording transactions by hand in paper volumes will always be a necessary element of bookkeeping.

Perhaps more importantly, understanding the underlying foundation of how paper journals and ledgers function and their main purpose in keeping accurate transaction records will give you a better understanding of professional bookkeeping. Digital technology has provided the means to automate many of these functions; however, the basic practice of professional bookkeeping remains the same. Attempting to take shortcuts by using financial management software without first understanding GAAP-complaint bookkeeping practices can lead to potentially serious complications.

What is a Ledger?

	A	B	C	D	E	F	G	H	I	J	K
1	General ledger example										
2											
3	General ledger example codes										
4	Budget Line Codes				Project Codes						
5	Grants Disbursement		0		Organizational Management		1				
6	Staff		10		Editing Workshop		2				
7	Food		20		Education Programs		3				
8	Equipment		30		GLAM		4				
9	Travel		40		Communications		5				
10	External Contract		50								
11	Contract Labor		51								
12	Contract Services		52								
13											
14	What you see in the general ledger										
15	Date	Account	Payee or Payor		Memo			Amount	Budget	Project	
16	11/5/2014	Checking	Wikimedia Foundation		Grant for November workshop			$150.00	0	2	
17	11/10/2014	Checking	Smith Library		Snacks for November 2014 workshop			-$25.00	20	2	
18	11/10/2014	Checking	Smith Library		Projector rental for November 2014 workshop			-$10.00	30	2	
19	11/11/2014	Checking	Beatrice Rodriguez		Bookkeeping contractor			-$109.41	52	1	
20	11/12/2014	Checking	Chen Repair Services		Fix damaged screen			-$62.25	30	1	
21	11/14/2014	Checking	Igor Flintrov		Salary for November 2014 workshop			-$113.18	51	2	
22	11/14/2014	Checking	Igor Flintrov		Salary for education programs support			-$540.73	51	3	
23	11/17/2014	Checking	Wikimedia Foundation		Return excess grant funds			-$1.82	0	2	
24											
25	Calculating the total costs for November 2014 workshop										
26		Salary	-$113.18								
27		Snacks	-$25.00								
28		Projector rental	-$10.00								
29		Total	-$148.18	The formula for this "Total" cell is =SUM(D26,D28)							
30											
31	Cost-effectiveness measures for the November 2014 workshop										
32					Number	Cost per each					
33		New editors			15	-$9.88	The formula for this "Cost per each" cell is =IFERROR($D$29/E33, "Not applicable")				
34		New articles			4	-$37.05	The formula for this "Cost per each" cell is =IFERROR($D$29/E34, "Not applicable")				
35		Files created			36	-$4.12	The formula for this "Cost per each" cell is =IFERROR($D$29/E35, "Not applicable")				
36		Edits made			207	-$0.72	The formula for this "Cost per each" cell is =IFERROR($D$29/E36, "Not applicable")				
37		Quality images included in new files			2	-$74.09	The formula for this "Cost per each" cell is =IFERROR($D$29/E37, "Not applicable")				
38		Valued images included in new files			0	Not applicable	The formula for this "Cost per each" cell is =IFERROR($D$29/E38, "Not applicable")				
39		Featured pictures included in new files			0	Not applicable	The formula for this "Cost per each" cell is =IFERROR($D$29/E39, "Not applicable")				

Figure 6: Free Image

In bookkeeping, a ledger is a book or record of financial accounts, with transaction data taken from the journal, then re-organized with all transaction entries sorted by account type rather than transaction date. Also called a general ledger, this record of accounts is organized according to the five main types of accounts – asset accounts; liability accounts; equity accounts; revenue accounts; and expense accounts.

The ledger is the centerpiece of the entire accounting cycle. Chapter 3 discussed how the chart of accounts (COA) lists all of the accounts, by type, that a company uses to keep track of its financial records. The general ledger represents all activity in every account listed in the COA. Every account listed in the COA will always have a balance, and that balance can be found by looking at the transaction records listed in the general ledger. So, if an employee wants to know the current available balance in petty cash, the general ledger will provide that information.

All the accounts listed in the COA are presented in the ledger in a standardized format the accommodates double-entry bookkeeping. Standard paper ledgers all use a T-Account entry that allows the bookkeeper to enter a debt and a credit for every transaction.

The following examples show how T-accounts are used to record transaction in a general ledger. In the first example, an expense account (rent) and a liability account (accounts payable) are debited and credited; in the second example, liability account (accounts payable) and an asset account (cash) are debited and credited. Even if your general ledger is kept in a computer database, the visual interface you use to enter account transaction information is likely to appear as a T-account.

Rent Expense					Accounts Payable			
Debit		Credit			Debit		Credit	
Date	Amt	Date	Amt		Date	Amt	Date	Amt
7/01	$10,000.00						7/01	$10,000.00
Bal $10,000.00							Bal $10,000.00	

Accounts Payable					Cash			
Debit		Credit			Debit		Credit	
Date	Amt	Date	Amt		Date	Amt	Date	Amt
7/06	$10,000.00						7/06	$10,000.00
Bal $10,000.00							Bal $10,000.00	

Here is another example of how T-accounts in a general ledger are used to allow a bookkeeper to record changes to the balance of an asset account, in this case a company's cash account:

Acct 101	CASH ON HAND		Balance
	Debits	Credits	(DR Bal)
1-Sep-14			$6,040
5-Sep-14	$4,200	$1,180	$9,060
6-Sep-14	$5,800		$14,860
6-Sep-14	$1,200		$16,060

Why Use a Ledger?

The general ledger provides comprehensive transaction information, including transaction history and its effect on the current balance for that category of account. As a result, because the general ledger places transactions into the proper accounting context, the ledger is used as the most authoritative source of financial information for a company. In a GAAP-compliant accounting system, there are generally five steps in the accounting cycle:

1. Business transactions occur.
2. Transactions are recorded as entries in journals.
3. Journal entries are transferred to ledgers.
4. Trial balances are created using the information in ledgers.
5. Ledgers are used to create financial statements.

Although ledgers do not enter the accounting cycle until the third step, they serve several extremely important functions:

- They allow bookkeepers and accountants to ensure the balances of every account in the COA are accurately adjusted to reflect the most recent transactions.

- They allow the accounting team, by creating trail balances, to ensure that all debts and credits for each account are equal. This step allows the accounting team to locate and correct bookkeeping errors prior to ending the fiscal year.

- They provide the source of the information that is presented in annual financial statements.

Modern corporations that employ large numbers of people in many locations, all of whom communicate using digital communication tools, may engage in transactions and record journal entries around-the-clock. This king of high-volume business activity presents even greater opportunities for bookkeeping errors, lost revenue and profitability, and potentially catastrophic accounting and tax liability concerns. By using a general ledger to maintain accurate account balances, those same digital tools can be used to ensure accountability and accuracy and increase the overall efficiency and effectiveness of the bookkeeping system.

The Nitty-Gritty About Journals and Ledgers

The previous sections' discussion general ledgers included references to financial journals. Financial journals are related to ledgers, but they are separate records that serve an entirely different purpose. As mentioned earlier in this book, the purpose of bookkeeping is to record every transaction in which a business engages. Financial statements provide the final accounting of these records for any given period of time, and these records are derived directly from the information maintained in the general ledger.

However, business transactions rarely follow such a neat and organized pattern, so bookkeepers must have a way of keeping track of transactions as they occur. This is the second step of the accounting cycle, and financial journals are used to maintain these records.

Like general ledgers, general journals traditionally take the form of paper-based notebooks or bound volumes. They contain page after page of transaction entries, all listed in chronological order. Because the journal is the place where transactions are first recorded, they are sometimes called the book of original entry. A journal entry will include detailed information about the transaction, such as the date, the accounts that should be debited and credited, and a description of the purpose of the transaction. Depending on the size and complexity of the company, the bookkeeping department may require the use of several types of journals, each designated for specific purposes – for example, purchase transaction journals, cash receipt journals, sales transaction journals, etc. Companies who use specialized journals may also utilize a general journal to record less frequently occurring transactions, like depreciation or interest.

One of the primary differences between journals and ledgers is that the information is journals is entered chronologically and by individual transaction. This information would require a lot of additional analysis to produce financial statements or to ensure that the accounts are all balanced; however, this format data entry allows bookkeepers and accountants to locate individual transactions more easily, and this feature can be very important to the overall effort to maintain accurate, balanced accounts.

For example, consider that the general ledgers provide the most authoritative view of all account information – the ledger shows the relationship of account balances to transactions. Before creating financial statements, the general ledger is used to create trial balances that can allow an accountant to determine whether the accounts are balanced – i.e., that credit and debits are equal across all accounts and account types. The importance of journals becomes apparent when accounts are out of balance. Although the ledger may indicate where the imbalance occurs, the journal holds the information about each individual transaction. This information can allow financial regulators and accountants to locate the source of the inaccuracy, correct the imbalance, and close the books at the end of the fiscal period.

The following is an example of how chronological entries may appear in a financial journal:

Date	Account Name	Debit	Credit
Feb 1, 2018	Cash	100,750	
	Bonds Payable		100,000
	Interest Payable		750
Feb 28, 2018	Interest Expense	750	
	Interest Payable		750
Mar 31, 2018	Interest Expense	750	
	Interest Payable		750
Apr 30, 2018	Interest Expense	750	
	Interest Payable		750
May 31, 2018	Interest Expense	750	
	Interest Payable		750
Jun 30, 2018	Interest Expense	750	
	Interest Payable		750
Jun 30, 2018	Interest Payable	4,500	
	Cash		4,500
Jul 31, 2018	Interest Expense	750	
	Interest Payable		750
Aug 31, 2018	Interest Expense	750	
	Interest Payable		750
Sep 30, 2018	Interest Expense	750	
	Interest Payable		750
Oct 31, 2018	Interest Expense	750	
	Interest Payable		750
Nov 30, 2018	Interest Expense	750	
	Interest Payable		750
Dec 31, 2018	Interest Expense	750	
	Interest Payable		750
Dec 31, 2018	Interest Payable	4,500	
	Cash		4,500

How to Input Data into a Ledger

Generally, transaction records should not be entered directly into an account ledger. The journal is the book of original entry, and this where all transaction records should begin. This distinction is easier to maintain for companies who use paper records. Traditional bookkeeping methods require the use of physically different books, and each book will have pages that are designed for different types of account entries. For example, the following is an example of a blank page from a financial journal. Notice how the page is specifically designed to accept chronological entries of transactions, with a description and an indication of whether it should be entered into the ledger as a debit or credit:

GENERAL JOURNAL

DATE	ACCOUNT NAME	DEBIT	CREDIT

By contrast, the following sample of a T-account page from a ledger looks completely different. The ledger page is designed to accept only entries affecting accounts receivable. The date of the transaction, space to indicate the type of transaction, and the amount the account should be debited or credited. The specific information entered into the T-account page is taken from the journal, where it was originally recorded.

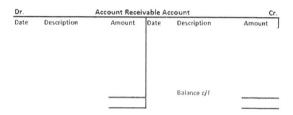

Of course, even companies that still maintain paper-based records usually use some type of bookkeeping software to help make entries more accurate, consistent, and traceable. For the most part, advances in bookkeeping technology have made the job of maintaining accurate records easier, more efficient, and less prone to error. However, automation has also resulted in some fundamental changes to the way bookkeeping entries may be made.

The primary difference between paper-based bookkeeping and automated bookkeeping is that paper-based records require physically different books to record transactions, while computer software may incorporate both journals and ledgers into the same program. This arrangement simplifies the concepts of journals and ledgers; in fact, many software applications do not even use the concepts of journals and ledgers, opting instead for a variety of user-interface windows that allow for various types of data entry functions. Although the software may make a distinction about the database in which certain data is stored based on the form or window used to enter the information, bookkeeping personnel who have been trained exclusively in these environments may believe that all transaction records are entered directly into the ledger. Although this confusion may not affect the ability of the bookkeeper to enter accurate data, understanding that journals and ledgers provide two different methods of recording business transactions is important when it is time to balance the books and produce accurate financial statements. The following are some of the fundamental difference between journal and ledgers:

Journals vs. Ledgers		
	Journal	Ledger
Definition	Journals are used as the first point of recording a financial transaction.	Ledgers use a T-format to record credits and balances by account type and supply date for financial statements.
Importance	The accuracy of journals is more important. The accuracy of the ledger depends on the accuracy of the journal.	The ledger depends on the transactions in the journal to produce financial statements.
Format	Simple format, date, descriptions, and transaction amount.	More complex accounting input, with account type and debits and

		credits for both sides
Alternate title	The book of original entry.	The book of second entry.
Entry terminology	Entering transactions in a journal is called journalizing.	Entering transactions in a ledger is called posting.
Method of record-keeping	Chronological	According to account
Balancing	Journals do not need to be balanced.	Ledgers must be balanced.

Different Types of Ledgers

As discussed throughout this section journals and ledgers each serve important roles in maintaining accurate and reliable records of any business's transaction details. The general principles of bookkeeping apply across the board regardless of what type of journal or ledger you use, or whether you are utilizing a digital software or a paper-based system. However, there are still many differences among the many types of ledgers and journals companies may use. There are three types of ledgers used in professional bookkeeping:

- General ledger
- Debtors ledger
- Creditors ledger

General Ledger

The general ledger (GL), as discussed above, contains all the transactions of the business, organized according to the five standard account types – assets, liabilities, equities, revenue, and expenses. Some companies that use a general ledger may also incorporate into the main ledger additional sub-ledgers, such as a nominal ledger or a private ledger. The nominal ledger contains transaction information for accounts that are less directly involved in the main function of the business – for example, salaries, rent, office supplies, insurance, and depreciation. The private ledger contains transaction information that is confidential, such as information about salaries and capital investments.

Debtors' Ledger

The debtors' ledger is also known as a sales ledger. These types of ledgers are used to record all transactions relating to customers who have purchased goods or services on credit. Companies who have the capacity to extend credit will maintain a debtors' ledger. This ledger will contain information about the total sum of money owed to the business. Accounts will be organized into categories such as Accounts Receivable, Trade Debtors, and Sundry Debtors. Traditionally, accounts in these types of ledger are organized alphabetically, although modern software has enabled a variety of search and sort functions.

Creditors' Ledger

The creditors' ledger records all transaction information related to sellers from whom goods or services have been purchased on credit. This ledger will contain information such as the total sum of money owed by a business to all individuals and organizations from whom they have made purchases that have not yet been paid. Account types in a creditors' ledger may include Accounts Payable, Trade Creditors, and Sundry Creditors. The values for each account of the creditors' ledger will appear in the appropriate area of the balance sheet when the accountant creates the trial balance.

Chapter 6: Essential Guide to Bookkeeping

The first five chapters of this book have covered many of the basic concepts of standardized, GAAP-compliant bookkeeping. By now, you should be feeling much more comfortable thinking about the basic skills and concerns you will have to address to ensure your company's bookkeeping is accurate, reliable, consistent, and up to professional standards. If you are assembling a bookkeeping system for yourself or for a client company, having a solid foundation in bookkeeping fundamentals is important.

This chapter pulls all that information together to give you an overview of everything you should consider before making any decisions about hiring a bookkeeper, building a system, or outsourcing your bookkeeping needs. The information in this chapter is divided into three sections:

- Startup Considerations
- Procedures During the Fiscal Period

- Procedures for the End of the Fiscal Period

Figure 7: Free Image

Startup Considerations

The bookkeeping and accounting system that any company uses should represent a long-term commitment resulting from a methodical and thorough examination of the company's current size and complexity, as well as its prospects and plans for future growth and development. One of the most important aspects in which accurate and reliable bookkeeping shows its value is tax filing. Depending on the size and complexity of your business concerns, the Internal Revenue Service (IRS) may require that you indicate which type of accounting and bookkeeping system your company uses; making changes to these agreements can be time-consuming, costly, and difficult, so it pays to think things through ahead of time. In addition, you; your investors and shareholders; your customer base; potential future investors; lenders; and financial regulators may request an examination or even an audit of your books. Producing reliable financial statements requires a disciplined and consistent method of bookkeeping so that changes in profit, loss, and equity over time can be more effectively and easily tracked. Thus, by choosing a bookkeeping and accounting system that is most appropriate for your business venture, you will be taking the right steps toward ensuring successful and profitable business administration.

Choosing a Bookkeeping System

As discussed earlier in this book, there are two recognized systems of GAAP-compliant bookkeeping: single-entry and double-entry. We will explore the pros and cons of both systems in this section. We will also discuss the strengths and weaknesses of online, web-based, and digital bookkeeping systems.

Single-entry Bookkeeping

A single-entry bookkeeping system is the most informal of all bookkeeping systems. If you have a checking account, the check register is a great example of single-entry bookkeeping. All the transactions in the check registry provide information about only the one checking account. Whether the transaction is a deposit resulting for a business transaction; from a personal or professional investment; from a business or personal loan; or from interest paid on the account or dividends received from investments in securities, all the transactions are listed chronologically, with a small space for description of the transaction, and a column on the right to show how the transaction affected the balance in the account.

Withdrawals are tracked the same way – whether a withdrawal results from a direct withdrawal from the bank for personal or business use; for payment of a bill for operating expenses for your business; form a purchase made for equipment or office supplies; from payments for loans, interest, or taxes; or from the purchase of investments, all the transactions will be listed chronologically; again with a small space for a description of the transaction; and a column on the right to show how the transaction affected the balance.

This method of bookkeeping is fairly straightforward and can be an effective means of showing accurately where money comes in and goes out each month. However, with the prevalence of online banking, we have all encountered the difficulty of keeping track of all transactions in a simple check register. Previous top widespread access to online banking, most deposit transactions were made in person at the bank, and most withdrawals were conducted by mailed checks. This level of control over financial activity made the single-entry system a more viable option for individuals and businesses over a much broader range of business contexts. The contemporary environment requires a reassessment of whether a single-entry system is right for you.

Advantages:

- Single-entry bookkeeping uses a simple and easy-to-understand method of keeping track of transactions.
- Small businesses that have only one major financial account may be able to save time and expense by using this system effectively.
- A single-entry system can be adapted for larger companies by creating separate single-entry systems for each business account.

Disadvantages:

- Single-entry systems do not provide a means of including detailed financial reporting.
- Bookkeeping errors can be very difficult to locate and usually involve reconciling bookkeeping records with bank statements.
- Single-entry systems do not provide an effective means of creating projections of future financial performance.
- Single-entry systems generally track only cash accounts. Other assets, as well as liabilities, equity, income, and expenses go unreported in these systems.

Double-entry Bookkeeping

Especially in a globalized, digital environment, it is common even for small, local businesses to have many accounts with different suppliers, service providers, and customers, often from different locations and even different countries. In addition, the increasingly self-service nature of investing and business administration can mean that even small businesses may have to take on considerably greater responsibility than in previous eras. Regardless, the larger and more complex your business, the more likely a double-entry system will allow you to consistently maintain reliable books. Most companies use the double-entry system.

In the section above, we used the analogy of a check register to describe the single-entry system. Using a double-entry system, the transactions in the previous example represent only half of the entire bookkeeping process. For example, if you made a deposit into your checking account for payments received from customers for good and services sold, the record of the deposit into the checking account (a single-entry) is only half of the transaction record; in order to balance the books, there needs to be a second-entry is a corresponding account. The idea behind double-entry systems is that putting money into one account necessarily means that money was taken from another account and vice-versa. Double-entry bookkeeping allows you to show both sides of the transaction. So, when a company makes a deposit resulting from sales, revenue can be credited for the same amount the checking account was debited, which results in a balanced record of the transaction. Similarly, if the business owner pays an outstanding bill for shipping, the double-entry system will record a credit to the checking account and a debit to the accounts payable.

Advantages:

- Provides a more complete system of recording all of a company's financial transactions, not just deposits and withdrawals to the main checking account.

- Provides a means of producing accurate and reliable financial statements.
- Provides an effective means of pinpointing internal accounting errors.
- Provides a means of accurately assessing a company's financial condition.

Disadvantages:

- Double-entry bookkeeping is more complex and may take more time to learn.

Choosing an Accounting Method

As there are two officially recognized methods of bookkeeping, so there are two officially recognized methods of accounting:

- Cash accounting
- Accrual accounting

Also similar to bookkeeping methods, choosing the most appropriate type of accounting method for your business will involve an assessment of the size and complexity of your business. This section examines the two different types of accounting methods, including advantages and disadvantages.

Cash Accounting

Cash accounting is fairly straightforward. It is called cash accounting because transactions are only recorded at the time cash changes hands. For example, in a business that uses cash-based accounting, a sale is recorded in the books at the time payment is received from the customer. Similarly, expenses are only recorded at the time the business actually makes a payment for a purchase or to pay a bill.

Advantages and Disadvantages:

Small businesses, such as sole proprietorships and limited partnerships, often use a cash accounting system, particularly when they do not have any inventory. The clear advantage to the cash accounting system is that it provides a very simple and straightforward method of recognizing when revenue has been received and when expenses have been paid. In addition, when using a cash accounting system, businesses do not pay taxes on income until is received.

However, a disadvantage is that using a cash accounting system does not allow a business to match its revenue and expenses in time. For example, if a construction business wins a contract in January and completes it in June, revenue is recorded in June when payment is received, even though the contract was signed in January. Similarly, if the same business receives an insurance bill due in quarterly installment, the expense is only recorded when the payments are made, rather than as an annual expense. the in its rent of $1,000 per month for the entire year in January, it would have to record a $12,000 expense in January, rather than distributing the payments throughout the year.

Accrual Accounting

Accrual accounting is more complex. It is called accrual accounting because transactions are recorded at the time they are earned or incurred, rather than when they are paid for. For example, consider a construction business that uses accrual accounting. The business may make a sale in January, but the contract may not be completed until June. Using accrual accounting, the business can record the sale in January, rather than waiting until June. Similarly, a company using accrual accounting records all the money it owes as current transactions in accounts payable, rather than waiting to record each bill as it is paid.

if the same business prepays rent on its facilities for the entire year in January, each of the monthly rent payments can be recorded as paid for the entire upcoming year, even though each of the rental installments may not yet have been deposited by the property manager.

Advantages and Disadvantages:

The accrual method is generally used by larger business. In fact, if a business generates over $5 million in annual revenue, the IRS requires that they use accrual accounting. The clear advantage to the accrual accounting system is that it provides a more accurate picture of the company's financial condition by allowing a business to match its revenue and expenses in time. For example, if a construction business wins a contract in January and completes it in June, revenue in an accrual system is recorded in January when the contract is signed, rather than waiting for payment in June, when the work is completed. Similarly, a company using accrual accounting can record at the beginning of the year the total amount of an annual insurance bill due in quarterly installment, rather than waiting to submit payments once a quarter.

To illustrate how this difference can affect the assessment of a company's financial picture, imagine that the construction company who won the contract in January wanted to apply for a business loan. Using cash accounting, a lender may be less willing to invest in the business because they cannot show earnings for the recently signed contract.

Similarly, a business using cash accounting that prepays its rent of $1,000 per month for the entire year in January would have to record a $12,000 expense in January, with no rent payments for the rest of the year; accrual accounting would allow the same business to distribute the expense throughout the year. Although the total rent expense for the year is the same, anyone examining the cash flow statement for either company at any given time may get a skewed picture of the company's overall performance.

Changing Accounting Methods

Cash accounting allows businesses to defer taxes by delaying the deposit of revenue. This may appeal to many businesses, particularly when they have large earnings at the end of the year. However, to avoid artificially inflated or deflated financial statements that can affect the health of the market, the IRS requires all businesses to state which type of accounting method they use. You also have to notify the IRS if you decide to change your accounting method by filing a Form 3115.

Here is a summary of the differences between the cash and accrual accounting:

Cash Accounting	Accrual Accounting
Recognizes revenue at the time it is received.	Recognizes revenue at the time it is earned (i.e., when an invoice or contract is completed),
Recognizes expenses at the time they are paid.	Recognizes expenses at the time they are billed (i.e., when the company receives an invoice).
Taxes are deferred on revenue that has not yet been received.	Taxes must be paid on revenue and accounts receivable.
Mostly used by small businesses and sole proprietors with no inventory.	Required for businesses with revenue over $5 million.

Procedures During the Fiscal Period

Now that you have decided on a bookkeeping system and an accounting method, the real work of recording your company's transactions can begin. There are a ton of resources available wherever you look – television, radio, print, and online service companies and independent operators all know there is money to be made in the gig economy simply by providing helpful advice and guidance in the day-to-day operation of a small business. A lot of these sources provide valuable information, but not all of it is dependable. This section will provide a general overview of some of the most important concerns you should be addressing as you establish an effective and reliable bookkeeping system.

Tracking Income and Expenses

Before you even think about producing or analyzing financial statements or tax documents, you need to establish a system of recording your day-to-day expenses. The law does not specify exactly how you should go about the process of recording your daily transactions and receipts or compiling your monthly or annual financial records. However, there are established bookkeeping and accounting methods that you must use. The best way to begin formulating a bookkeeping system that works for you is to simply visit your local office supply store and buy a journal and a ledger to record your daily transactions. A single-entry cash accounting system can be an effective method of tracking expenses for a small startup company; if your company grows, you can adapt the bookkeeping and accounting methods to address those changes. If you have a business checking account, you may also use a business checkbook to record transactions.

The following is a list of all the types of books that may be required for a recordkeeping system for a small business:

- business checkbook
- journals to record the following:
  - daily summary of cash receipts
  - check disbursements journal

- ○ monthly summary of cash receipts
- ○ depreciation worksheet
- ○ employee compensation record
- a general ledger to record how the transactions in the journals are reflected in the business checking account.

Alternatively, you may use computer software to track your expenses and receipts. These software programs are usually fairly easy to use and may require little knowledge of bookkeeping to begin making entries. Chapter 10 examines QuickBooks and other online and digital bookkeeping applications.

Organizing Documents

Once you have decided how you will be recording your business's daily, weekly, and monthly transactions, you must have some idea of what types of expenses you will be tracking. The importance of keeping receipts, invoices, paid bills, deposit slips, canceled checks, and bank statements is that they provide support for the numbers you enter into your bookkeeping and accounting system. The accuracy of this information is important because it affects the accuracy of the information in your tax returns and can help you resolve inquiries from auditors, the IRS, as well as support claims of creditworthiness on loan applications.

The following are the types of transaction records you should be recording, separated into 4 main categories:

- Gross receipts. All receipts of business income resulting from sales of goods or services fall under the category of gross receipts. Transaction records should show dates, amounts received and sources. Examples of gross receipts include:

  - cash register tapes
  - bank deposit slips
  - receipt book slips

- invoices
- credit card charge slips and receipts
- IRS forms 1099-MISC

• Inventory. Inventory refers to all items purchased and resold to customers, including raw materials used to produce finished items. Records of inventory transactions should show the amount paid and an indication that it was purchased for inventory. Inventory records may include:

- cancelled checks
- cash register receipts
- credit/debit card sales receipts
- invoices from suppliers

• Expenses. Records of all costs incurred to run your business (except for inventory) should go here. These records should show the amount and date paid with some indication that it was a business-related expense. Transaction records may include:

- cancelled checks
- cash register receipts
- credit/debit card sales receipts
- account statements for service suppliers

- invoices

- petty cash receipts for per diem expenses

• Assets. As discussed earlier, assets include all property owned by the business that has some type of practical value for the business. Asset records should not only show purchase price but also track depreciation and losses or gains when the assets are sold. Any of the following documents may show this information:

- purchase and sales invoices

- real estate closing statements

- canceled checks or other transaction receipts

Organizing Deductions

When you file income tax at the end of the year, you should be able to deduct the expenses associated with running your business from the total revenue earned. When you report a lower total revenue, you will be less in taxes. The following are the types of business expenses the IRS allows you to deduct on our tax returns:

- Business start-up costs. The types of costs associated with start-ups vary depending on the type of business but may include:

  ○ advertising

  ○ travel

  ○ surveys

  ○ training

  ○ asset purchases

- Depreciation. If you purchased assets that will last longer than one year, you can claim as start-up expenses. However, you can claim the value of depreciation for such assets. Typically, asset depreciation is claimed for the following types of assets:

  ○ office furniture

  ○ buildings

  ○ equipment and machinery

- Business use of home. If your home is your principal place of business, you may be able to claim certain tax deductions, but you will have to provide documentation that shows:

  ○ what business services are performed at your home.

- how your home has been converted to business use.

- Car and truck expenses. Keeping accurate records of your car and truck usage can also help you find ways to save money. The following types of business-related travel expenses are deductible:

  - depreciation
  - lease payments
  - registration
  - garage rent
  - licenses
  - repairs
  - gas
  - oil
  - tires
  - insurance
  - parking fees
  - tolls

Invoicing Customers

One of the primary transaction records you will be maintaining is sales revenue, under gross receipts. As a result, ensuring that your business has a reliable system of invoicing is essential.

- ## Standard invoices

For your general bookkeeping needs, you can purchase not only journals and ledgers at your local office supply store but also invoice books. You may also wish to create company invoices that match your company letterhead. Regardless, you should record every invoice you send in one journal, and all paid invoices in another journal, with monthly balances transferred to the ledger as either revenue or accounts receivable.

• Electronic Invoices

Chapter 10 discusses QuickBooks and other digital and web-based bookkeeping and accounting systems. Many – if not all – of these systems offer some type of invoicing function. Many businesses choose this system because the invoicing feature will also automatically record the invoice in accounts receivable and provide a method of tracking sent invoices and entering payments when they are received by customers. Other online money transferring applications like PayPal also offer invoicing functions. PayPal and other web-based payment systems can be adapted for business uses. The invoicing features are fairly flexible and allow for customized invoice design, as well as fairly complex reporting systems that can allow business to keep track of invoices sent and payments received. If you use online invoicing as part of your business's bookkeeping and invoicing system, make sure you incorporate all activity associated with your business into your daily, weekly, and monthly bookkeeping records.

Procedures for the End of the Fiscal Period

Throughout the fiscal year, much of your time and effort will be spent producing the goods and services for you your business. At the end of the year, you will have to file your business income taxes. You will also have the opportunity to balance the books and create reports to assess the performance of your business and make decisions about how you intend to move forward.

During the course of the year, you will have to dedicate some of that time to recording all transactions that affect your business's financial condition. The more disciplined, regular, and well-organized your bookkeeping system, the easier it will be for you to prepare end-of-cycle financial statements and records. This section will examine some of those areas in detail.

Closing the Books

"The books" are the records of your company's financial transactions. Whether you keep paper records, digital records, or a combination of both you will compile a lot of information in journals and ledgers as you keep track of your business's activities throughout the year. At the end of the year (or whichever period signals the end of a financial cycle for you), your bookkeeping and accounting team must "close the books." Closing the books means that all of your financial reporting for that period will be finalized. Once the books are closed, no further adjustments will be made to those records, although you will have to keep copies of those records on file for as many as 7 years after closing.

The purpose of closing the books is to ensure that all income and expenses have been accounted for accurately and that all transactions for the current period have been completed or otherwise accounted for. Closing the books also presents businesses with the opportunity to create financial statements that can provide insight into their company's performance, profitability, and efficiency.

Closing the books is a multi-step process. Each of those steps is highlighted below:

1. Transfer journal entries to the general ledger.

Depending on your method of bookkeeping and accounting, you may transfer journal entries into the ledger at the end of each week, each month, each quarter, or at the end of the year. Generally, for companies that keep paper records, transferring journal entries into the ledger once a month is common practice.

If your company uses bookkeeping software, your journal entries may be automatically transferred into the ledger at the point of entry. Alternatively, your software may have features that allow you to manually tell the program when to transfer journal entries into the ledger, or to automate the data transfer.

2.   Compile a Preliminary Trial Balance

A trial balance is a worksheet that can be created manually or using bookkeeping software. The trial balance reflects the totals of all the debits and all the credits in all of the accounts included in the ledger. The purpose of the trial balance is to ensure all account entries in the journals and the ledger up to the end of the reporting period were entered accurately by checking the math to see if the debits and credits have equal balances.

To create a preliminary trial balance:

- Add up all the debit and credit transaction totals in every account in the ledger. To balance a ledger account, total all the debits and credits to each account. The resulting totals will be either a debit or credit balance.

- Next, prepare a trial balance worksheet with three columns – one column lists account names from the ledger; one column lists debit balances; and one column lists credit balances.

- Third, write the name of each account from the ledger and its total credit or debit balance in the worksheet. Following is an example of a trial balance worksheet:

Trial Balance
XYZ Trading
as at 30 June 2010

General Ledger Accounts	[Dr.-Debit]	[Cr.-Credit]
Cash at bank	10,000	
Inventory	40,000	
Vehicles	30,000	
Fixtures & Fittings	32,000	
Accounts Receivable	15,000	
Credit Cards payable		12,000
Accounts Payable		15,000
Bank Loan		50,000
Sales		175,000
Purchases	60,000	
Advertising	5,000	
Wages	65,000	
Rent	15,000	
Electricity	5,000	
Owners Capital		25,000
TOTAL	**277,000**	**277,000**

- Fourth, add the balances in the debit column and write the total at the bottom; then, add the balances in the credit column and write that total at the bottom. If the total debits equal the total credits, your books are balanced.

3. Add adjusting journal entries.

Accumulation and depreciation should be tracked in a separate journal. These figures should be transferred to the ledger, then added to the trial balance worksheet.

4. Create an adjusted trial balance.

- After adding the figures for accumulation and depreciation, add the columns of debits and credits again.
- This is the adjusted trial balance. If the total at the bottom of the debit column is the same as the total of the credit column, your books are balanced and ready to close.

5. Make corrections.

- If the total debit and credit balances are not equal, you will have to locate the bookkeeping errors and make corrections. The following are some areas where errors commonly occur:
  - Mistakes transferring amounts from the ledger to the trial balance worksheet.
  - Errors in calculating balances of ledger accounts.
  - Incorrect amounts posted in the ledger from the journal.
  - Debited an account instead of crediting an account, or vice versa.
  - Error in entering a transaction in a journal.
- Once you have located the discrepancy and corrected the balance, run the trial balance again until the total debits and credits match.

| 6. | Generate financial statements. |

- Chapter 4 of this book discusses the three types of financial statements in greater detail:
  - Balance sheet. Remember, the balance sheet shows the company's total assets, liabilities, and equities at the time the report is created.
  - Income statement. The income statement shows how much profit the company generated over the previous accounting cycle by showing the total revenue left over after all expenses have been deducted.
  - Cash flow statement. Finally, the cash flow statement shows how the company generated profit – whether it was generated mostly from selling goods and services or resulted primarily for loans and investments.
- If your company uses bookkeeping software, generating reports and financial statements may be as easy as clicking on a button or selecting a "Create financial statements" option for a dropdown menu. However, the financial statements themselves will only be as valuable as the information in the

journals and ledgers from which the software application draws data to create the reports. For this reason, it is important to ensure that you complete all the preliminary steps before attempting to generate final reports.

- Alternatively, you may keep paper-based records. If this is the case, you can use or edit pre-designed templates for each of the three main types of financial statements, then transfer the data from the general ledger directly into the templates. The examples in Chapter 4 illustrate the types of templates that are widely available for this purpose. You can find blank templates using an internet search engine or at your local office supply store.

7.   Enter closing entries.

Revenue and expense accounts should be closed with zero balances. Remaining balances should be transferred to permanent accounts such as accounts payable or retained earnings.

8.   Generate a final trial balance.

The final trial balance will show the total debits and credits of all the accounts listed on the balance sheet for that accounting period.

Chapter 7: How to Set Up a Single-Entry Bookkeeping System

By now you have read about most of the basic principles involved in basic bookkeeping and accounting for small businesses. To review, the previous chapters have covered the following topics:

- Types of bookkeeping methods:

    - Single-entry
    - Double-entry

- Types of accounting methods:

    - Cash accounting
    - Accrual accounting

- Financial statements:

    - Balance sheets
    - Income statements

- Cash flow statements

- Basic recordkeeping:

  - Financial journals
  - General ledgers
  - Beginning and ending activities for the bookkeeping cycle

Most of these principles are easy enough to understand in theory. However, putting them into practice in your business can be a little more challenging. This chapter and the next will use case studies to illustrate specifically how a business owner can set up and start using a bookkeeping system. This chapter will focus on single-entry bookkeeping that uses cash accounting.

Case Study: Brown Computer Repair

Figure 8: Free Image

Let's assume that Alan and Mary Brown own a computer repair shop. Their business is a sole proprietorship that generates less than $5 million in revenue annually. In addition, because they provide repair services, their business does not maintain an inventory of items for resale. Instead, when a repair job requires additional parts, they order them for that specific contract only. Of course, they do maintain fixed assets that include equipment, office furniture, and other supplies necessary to run their business. The Browns have one part-time employee, Margaret O'Sullivan.

We will use the Browns' computer repair business to illustrate how a single-entry cash accounting system can be used to maintain accurate and reliable records of business transactions. Remember, this example is used for illustration purposes; in actual practice, your business may implement practices much different from this example.

Setting up the Cash Book

The cash book is a journal that records the cash sales, income, and payments made from the cash accounts of the business. The transactions are all recorded in the cash book in chronological order as they occur and balanced on a daily basis. At a regular interval – usually once a month – the results of the transactions recorded in the cash book will be posted to the appropriate cash account in the general ledger.

- ## Daily Summary of Cash Receipts

The Browns' cash book includes a Summary of Cash Receipts to record proceeds for all cash sales for each business day. Throughout the day, the Browns keep track of sales using printouts of online invoices paid, and cash register receipts from in-store sales. At the end of the business day, the Browns add all the money received through sales for that day, including sales tax, and record the amount in the space for total receipts for that day. In this example, the Browns also maintain a Petty Cash fund of $150.00, so they can make small cash purchases without having to access the business checking account. Whenever they make purchases out of the petty cash fund, they issue a receipt, which is included in the total cash receipts for the day. The amount petty cash spent, and the remaining amount in the fund are included in the daily balance. When the fund approaches $0.00, the Browns write check to Petty Cash and restore the find to a $150.00 balance. The check is recorded as a transaction in the Check Payments journal.

On January 7, the Browns totaled all their sales receipts for the day. Altogether, they generated $726.42 in cash sales, plus an additional $61.75 in sales tax. In addition, they had used $42.00 from the petty cash fund to buy cables and adapters. The total of all sales rescripts, plus petty cash receipts, is recorded in the Daily Summary of Cash Receipts in the cashbook, as follows:

Daily Cash Receipts

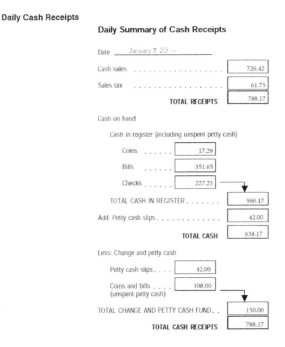

Daily Summary of Cash Receipts

Date _____ January 7, 20 — _____

Cash sales		726.42
Sales tax		61.75
TOTAL RECEIPTS		788.17

Cash on hand

Cash in register (including unspent petty cash)

Coins	17.29	
Bills	351.65	
Checks	227.23	
TOTAL CASH IN REGISTER		596.17
Add: Petty cash slips		42.00
TOTAL CASH		638.17

Less: Change and petty cash

Petty cash slips	42.00	
Coins and bills . . . . (unspent petty cash)	108.00	
TOTAL CHANGE AND PETTY CASH FUND . .		150.00
TOTAL CASH RECEIPTS		788.17

- ## Monthly Summary of Cash Receipts

Next, the total daily cash receipts recorded in the Daily Summary of Cash Receipts is transferred to the Monthly Summary of Cash Receipts for that day. In the example below, total cash receipts before and after taxes are shown for every business day in January. The column at the far right also shows the record of total deposits made into the business checking account.

Monthly Summary of Cash Receipts

Year 20—   Month January

Day	Net Sales	Sales Tax	Daily Receipts	Deposit
3	413.12	35.12	448.24	
4	217.23	18.47	235.70	
5	287.26	24.42	311.68	
6	322.42	27.41	349.83	
7	726.42	61.75	788.17	
8	114.22	9.71	123.93	2,257.55
10	108.24	9.22	117.46	
11	33.68	2.86	36.54	154.00
12	322.58	27.42	350.00	
13	522.12	44.38	566.50	
14	227.89	19.37	247.26	
15	67.42	5.73	73.15	1,236.91
17	587.24	49.92	637.16	
18	200.58	17.05	217.63	854.79
19	487.32	41.42	528.74	
20	128.54	10.93	139.47	
21	365.24	31.05	396.29	1,064.50
22	287.12	24.41	311.53	
24	198.47	16.87	215.34	526.87
25	318.02	27.03	345.05	
26	77.21	6.56	83.77	
27	322.58	27.42	350.00	778.82
28	187.54	15.94	203.48	
29	118.29	10.06	128.35	
31	210.12	17.86	227.98	559.81
TOTALS	6,850.87	582.38	7,433.25	7,433.25

When the Browns close the books at the end of the year, the total of all monthly net sales will be used to calculate the annual income for the business. Remember that only net sales can be used to calculate income; the income tax collected must be set aside in a taxes payable account, so all taxes collected can be paid to the state at the end of the accounting period.

Annual Summary of Cash Receipts				
Month	Net Sales	Sales Tax	Daily Receipts	Deposits
January	$6,850.87	$582.38	$7,433.25	$7,433.25
February	$7,587.42	$489.34	$8,076.76	$8,076.76
March	$6,687.22	$568.41	$7,255.63	$7,255.63
April	$5,988.35	$509.01	$6,497.36	$6,497.36
Totals	xxx	xxx	xxx	xxx

• Journal of Business Expenses

The Browns use another journal to record all the business expenses that are paid using the business checking account. The Monthly Check Disbursement Journal has columns for the day of the month, the check number, the party to whom the check is payable, and the amount.

The additional columns allow the Browns to specify what the funds are being used to pay for. For example, check #126 to AT&T pays for the monthly phone bill, so the total amount is recorded in the Telephone column. Other expenses, like Checks 125 and 133 to the Browns' employee show the amount of the payment that is used for payroll tax. And Check #24 to Petty Cash shows that some of the money was used to pay for postage, with the balance used to restore the balance in the petty cash fund.

The total amount of all checks written can be included in the ledger; the additional columns that specify how the funds were used can help the Browns isolate specific expenses, revenue, and taxes payable when they close their books at the end of the accounting cycle.

The example below illustrates how a check disbursement journal can be set up. In addition, the information in this monthly journal can be transferred into the annual ledger, as in the example above.

Check Disbursement Journal
Year: 20   Month: January

Day	Payable To	Check #	Amount	Materials	Payroll	Payroll taxes	Electricity	Rent	Telephone	Transportation	Owner Salary	Other Expenses	
3	City Hall	123	$35.00									Buisness License	$35.00
4	ABC Marketing and Sales	124	$150.00									Advertising	$150.00
5	Margaret O'Sullivan	125	$205.00		$250.00	-$45.00							
6	AT&T	126	$28.95						$28.95				
7	Downtown Auto	127	$275.00	$125.00								Labor	$150.00
8	Alan Brown	128	$250.00								$250.00		
8	Mary Brown	129	$250.00								$250.00		
9													
10	Central Electric	130	$47.52				$47.52						
11													
12													
13													
14													
15													
16	ABC Gas	131	$47.52							$47.52			
17													
18	City Parking	132	$75.00							$75.00			
19	Margaret O'Sullivan	133	$205.00		$250.00	-$45.00							
20													
21													
22													
23													
24	Petty Cash	134	$45.00									Postage	$3.00
25													
26													
27													
28	Acme Property Management	135	$325.00					$325.00					
29													
30													
31	State Franchise Tax Board	136	$582.38									Sales tax	$582.38
	Bank Fee		$12.00										$12.00
Totals			$2,533.37	$125.00	$500.00	$0.00	$47.52	$325.00	$28.95	$122.52	$500.00		$932.38

Finally, The Browns' single-entry cash accounting system will likely require them to reconcile their books with their bank statement each month to ensure there are no inaccurate entries. The Browns use the bank reconciliation form below to complete the following steps for this bookkeeping function, as follows:

1.   Mary Brown enters the bank statement balance of $2,426.52.

2.   Mary compares the deposits listed in the bank statement with the deposits shown in the checkbook. She sees that two deposits that appeared in the checkbook – one for $778.82 and another for $559.81 – did not appear on the bank statement. She enters the missing amounts on the bank reconciliation form and adds them to the bank statement balance. The subtotal is now $3,765.15.

3.   Next, Mary compares all the canceled checks with the check register and locates three outstanding checks totaling $218.62.   By subtracting this amount from the subtotal, she arrives at the adjusted balance of $3,546.53.

4.   Now, Mary enters the checkbook balance showing in the company's business checkbook.

5.   Mary locates an error that Alan made when he recorded a deposit of $683.42 that should have been $638.42. This is a difference of $45.00, which she subtracts from the checkbook balance. In addition, the bank service fee of $12.00 was not entered into the checkbook, so Mary deducts it here. The result is $3,546.53, which is the same amount listed in the adjusted balance in #3, above.

Bank Reconciliation

Bank Reconciliation as of:

Date _____January 31, 20 —_____

Closing balance shown on bank statement . . [2,426.52]

Add deposits not credited:

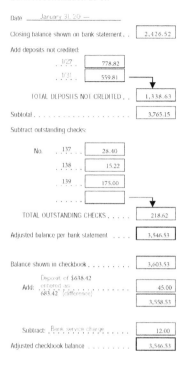

. . 1/27 . . [778.82]

. . 1/31 . . [559.81]

TOTAL DEPOSITS NOT CREDITED . . [1,338.63]

Subtotal . . . . [3,765.15]

Subtract outstanding checks:

No. . . 137 . . . [28.40]

. . 138 . . [15.22]

. . 139 . . [175.00]

. . . . . [ ]

TOTAL OUTSTANDING CHECKS . . . . . [218.62]

Adjusted balance per bank statement . . . . [3,546.53]

Balance shown in checkbook . . . . [3,603.53]

Deposit of $638.42
Add: entered as . . . . [45.00]
683.42 (difference)

[3,558.53]

Subtract: Bank service charge . . . . . [12.00]

Adjusted checkbook balance . . . . [3,546.53]

Chapter 8: How to Set Up a Double-Entry Bookkeeping System

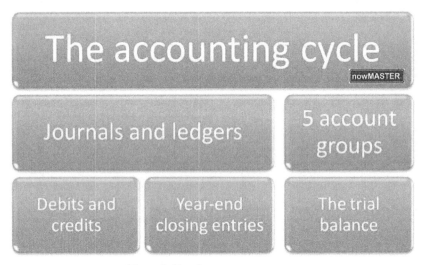

Figure 9: Free Image

The previous chapter illustrated how a small business owner can use a single-entry cash accounting system to record even a fairly complex array of transactions. Whether you are responsible for issuing payroll checks with tax deductions; loan payments; processing payments for sales of goods and services; or recording the daily costs associated with running your business, a well-designed single-entry cash accounting system can meet your needs.

Many people and businesses now use bookkeeping and accounting software. Bookkeeping and accounting software offers many advantages over paper-based bookkeeping systems. For example, most programs include error-checking functions and allow people with a limited knowledge of bookkeeping to jump right in without undergoing extensive training and certification. Bookkeeping programs also allow users to search for specific transactions that have been stored in the software's database and to create financial statements and reports fairly easily.

Bookkeeping software generally uses a double-entry system to record transactions. Although the software itself can make this more complex system of bookkeeping easier to manage, it's a good idea to have a basic understanding of how a double-entry system should be used to record business transactions. This section provides a step-by-step illustration of how to keep the books using a double-entry system.

Identifying and Classifying Accounting Source Documents

No matter what type of business transaction you want to record in your bookkeeping system, that transaction must be associated with some type of documentation. Make sure you have set up a system in which you have control over the documents you produce and receive.

Depending on the type of transaction, many people may receive a copy of the accounting source document, which may vary in complexity. Documents may be electronic files such as PDF or Word documents; they may be electronically produced paper documents, such as computer receipts; or they may be written paper documents. Regardless of what form the document takes or what type of transaction it represents, you should first ensure that all your accounting source documents contain all the following information:

- the transaction date
- the amount of the transaction
- the names of the people or companies involved in the transaction
- some type of reference number
- a description of the transaction

In addition, your accounting source documents may result from any of the following types of transactions:

- quotes from sellers of inventory or supplies

- orders from customers or clients with the details of what they are requesting from your business.

- Delivery dockets or bills of lading that include a description of all items purchased, along with costs, quantities, totals, taxes, and any other related costs.

- Sales and purchase invoices and receipts. These documents are similar to dockets but are issued when a sale is made and include the details of the goods or services purchased; any terms of payment that may have been agreed to; and amounts owed and/or paid.

- Credit and debit notes. These receipts are issued either when a customer returns an item. The seller's receipt of the transaction shows a reduction in the amount owed by the customers, so it is called a credit note; the customer's receipt for this transaction shows a reduction in the amount they owe the seller, so it is called a credit note.

- Payment remittances are issued by customers when they pay their invoices; they are also issued by businesses to let customers know their payments have been received.

Recording Daily Transactions

During the day-to-day operation of your business, you will complete many transactions. As a result, you will produce and receive many accounting source documents. The double-entry bookkeeping process starts with transferring the information contained in the documents to the bookkeeping journal. Chapter 7 provides an illustration of a daily and monthly cash receipt journal. A company that uses double-entry bookkeeping will have to use a different approach to record these transactions.

Setting Up Journals

Double-entry bookkeeping will use two types of journals:
- General journals
- Special journals
  - Sales journals
  - Cash receipts journals

- Sales return journals
- Purchase journals
- Cash payment journals
- Purchase return journals

The general journal serves as a business's main bookkeeping journal. Most transactions should be recorded in the general ledger. Special journals allow for more efficient and easier recording of transactions of a similar type.

General Journal

We will begin by illustrating how to record transactions in a general journal. Using the example in Chapter 7, we will show how the Browns would record payment for their telephone bill on January 6, which appears in the Monthly Check Disbursement record in Chapter 7.

First, you will need to create a blank page for general journal entries, with five columns:

				J1
Date	Description	Dr	Cr	Ref

Jan 06, 20---	Telephone	28.95		003
			28.95	001
	Telephone bill paid with Ck #126			

In this example, the method of recording the same transaction is very different:

- At the top, the page journal is identified as J1.
- The first description shows "Telephone," and indicates that the Telephone account in the main ledger should be debited.
- The second line is indented and shows that the "Checking" account in the ledger should be credited for the same amount.
- The Ref column can serve two purposes:

- By entering "P" in this column, the bookkeeper can indicate that the transaction has been posted to the ledger.
- Alternatively, the numbers in the Ref account in this example indicate the ledger account number to which these transactions should be posted – the telephone account is #003 in the Chart of Accounts; the Checking account is 001.

- The page number of the journal will be used as a reference in the ledger to show where the posted transaction is located in the journal.
- The next business transaction can be recorded directly beneath this transaction, after skipping one line in the journal.

Special Journals

To illustrate the difference between a general journal and
special journal, let's first create a hypothetical transaction in a
general journal that records a sale on credit. For example,
using the Browns' computer repair business, let's say they
sold a computer repair service to a walk-in customer. The
customer needed the repair done immediately and agreed to
send payment within 30 days of receiving the invoice. Here's
how the record would look in the general journal:

				J2
Date	**Description**	**Dr**	**Cr**	**Ref**
Jan 12, 20---	Accounts Receivable	225.00		002
			225.00	004
	Mr. Adams: Pmt. in 30 days.			

Because it can be difficult to enter every credit sale in the general journal, then transfer everything to the general ledger, and then make adjustments when accounts payable are converted to revenue or income, it may be easier to create a special journal that records only credit sales. If all the transactions in such a special journal result from credit sales, the bookkeeper eliminates the need to enter debit, credit, and description information for every transaction. Instead, a special journal can be created to record shorthand versions of these transactions:

					SJ1
Date	Account	Inv. No.	Terms	Ref	Amount
Jan 06	B. Barnes	2001	30 days	B	180.00
Jan 12	A. Adams	2002	60 days	A	225.00
Jan 22	H. Franklin	2003	30 days	H	210.00
Jan 31	Dr Accounts Receivable, Cr. Sales				615.00

Thus, in this special journal to record only this type of transaction:

- The "Description" field is replaced with an "Account" field that contains the customer's name.

- "Invoice" and "Terms" fields replace the Dr and Cr fields.

- The "Reference" field now refers to the account holder's first initial, rather than the account in the ledger.

- Credits and Debits are indicated at the bottom of the journal on the last day of the month, just before the information is transferred to the general journal and ledger.

Similar variations can be created for any type of specialized transaction that occurs frequently.

Transferring Journal Entries to the Ledger

Chapter 7 illustrated how the Browns' single-entry bookkeeping system tracked daily receipts and spending, then transferred the results to a monthly worksheet, and then transferred the monthly results to an annual summary.

Double-entry systems are similar, but they require the bookkeeper to transfer all the general and special journal entries into the general ledger, also using debits and credits to record every transaction twice.

Remember that the Chart of Accounts lists all of a company's accounts – assets, liabilities, equity, expenses, and revenue. In addition, three types of ledgers are used to record business transactions:

- A general ledger
- An accounts payable ledger
- An accounts receivable ledger

The general ledger is the main ledger for bookkeeping. Each account from the chart of accounts is assigned its own page in the general ledger. Accounts with many transactions may use several pages, but in no case should transactions form more than one account appear on the same page of the general ledger.

Next, transactions from the General Journal should be transferred to the appropriate page of the General Ledger. The following example shows a page from the Checking account in the General Ledger of the Browns' business:

Checking							001
Date	Description	Ref	Debit	Date	Description	Ref	Credit
Jan 01	Opening balance		3750.00	Jan 03		J2	67.00
Jan 07		J1	225.00	Jan 06		J1	28.95
Jan 24		J2	72.50	Jan 14		J1	88.00

General ledgers in a double-entry system share many common features:

- Notice the "T-account" structure, with debits recorded on the left and credits recorded on the right.
- The Date columns indicate the month for which transactions are being recorded.
- The debt columns on the left increase the balance in the checking account, so this is where deposits are posted.

- The credits on the right decrease the checking balance, so this is where withdrawals are posted. (Notice the Browns' telephone bill from January 06).

- The References field shows the page number of the journal from which the information was taken.

- Descriptions are recorded in the journals, so there is less of a need to record them in the ledger.

At the end of the month, the bookkeeper totals the amounts of debits and credits. Credits are subtracted from debits to calculate the closing balance. That figure is used as the new opening balance for the next month.

Accounts Payable and Accounts Receivable Ledgers

These types of ledgers are similar to the special journals that help the bookkeeper record specific types of transactions during the month. Accounts Payable ledgers help the bookkeeper to keep track of how much money a business owes its creditors; the Accounts Receivable ledger help the bookkeeper to keep track of how much money clients and customers owe the business.

Although they are called Accounts Payable and Accounts Receivable ledger, they are subsidiary ledgers. They are not used themselves in creating reports or financial statements. Instead, the balances in these two types of lagers are transferred to the corresponding accounts in the General Ledger. Following are two examples of Accounts Receivable Ledgers taken from the examples above:

B Barnes					B
Date		Ref	Debit	Credit	Balance
Jan 06	Terms 30	SJ1	180.00		180.00

A Adams					A
Date		Ref	Debit	Credit	Balance
Jan 12	Terms 60	SJ1	225.00		225.00

Accounts Payable ledgers are structured similarly, with the following features:

- The customer or client name in the upper left of the page.
- The page name on the upper right.
- The Ref field references the special journal from which the information was taken.

Double-entry Bookkeeping Example

To illustrate how the double-entry bookkeeping system works in practice, let's create a simple example using the Browns' computer repair shop as the business for whom we are keeping books. We will illustrate using two types of transactions:

- an income transaction;
- an expense transaction.

Then, we will show how those transactions should be recorded using:

- a journal
- a ledger
- a report

- ## Income transaction

On January 15, Alan Brown opens Brown Computer Repair at 8:00am. At 8:30, his first customer of the day, Mr. Gates, walks in. His customer requests a tune-up and virus removal for his laptop. Alan Brown writes the invoice and tells the customer the job will be completed by 3:00pm that day. The total cost is $125.95. The customer pays cash using a debit card from his bank. Alan Brown places the receipt from the debit card transaction in the bookkeeping file in the back office.

- ## Expense transaction

On January 17, Alan Brown receives the monthly electric bill for Brown Computer Repair. The bill is for $37.26 and shows the date of the bill, the description of charges, and the amount. Alan writes check #226 to the local electrical utility provider. He places the check in the mail and puts the check receipt from the check register, along with a copy of the bill, in the bookkeeping file in the back office.

At the end of the week, the bookkeeper processes all business transactions for the week in the following order:

1. enter transactions into journals;

2.   post journal entire sot ledgers;

3.   create reports.

- ## Journal entries

The bookkeeper's first task is to enter the transactions into the general journal. Journal entries are determined by the receipts and invoices and are entered chronologically, with a debit entry, a credit entry, and a description line. There should be a one-line space between entries. Here is how the journal entries looked for this week at Brown Computer repair:

				J1
Date	Description	Dr	Cr	Ref
Jan 15	Checking	125.95		
	Sales		125.95	

	Mr. Gates: Debit card pmt.			
Jan 17	Electric	37.26		
	Checking		37.26	
	January utility bill, Ck. #226			

• ## Posting to the Ledger

At the end of the month, the bookkeeper must post all the transactions recorded in the journal to the general ledger. There are two transactions to post for this example. The ledger is organized by account type, so the bookkeeper must identify which accounts in the general ledger he will have to access.

The income transaction shows a debit to the Checking account and a Credit to the Sales account. The expense transaction shows a debit to the Electricity account and a credit to the Checking account. So, the bookkeeper will have to post transactions to three different accounts in the ledger:

- Checking
- Sales
- Electricity

Here is how these three transactions look when the bookkeeper has completed posting them to the ledger:

Checking							001
Date	Description	Ref	Debit	Date	Description	Ref	Credit
Jan 01	Opening balance		3750.00	Jan 17		J1	37.26
Jan 15		J1	125.95				
Jan 31	Closing balance		88.69				

Sales							002
Date	Description	Ref	Debit	Date	Description	Ref	Credit
Jan 01	Opening balance		0.00	Jan 15	Mr. Gates: Debit purchase	J1	125.95
				Jan 31	Closing balance		125.95

Electricity							003
Date	Description	Ref	Debit	Date	Description	Ref	Credit
Jan 01	Opening balance		00.00				

Jan 17	Monthly bill	J1	37.26				
Jan 31	Closing balance		37.26				

- ## Preparing reports

Finally, the bookkeeper will prepare reports at the end of the accounting cycle. In this example, the bookkeeper will create a Balance sheet showing profit and loss. Obviously, this is a very simple example, but it illustrates how the accounting cycle progresses and how double-entry bookkeeping can make this process work:

Profit and Loss Statement

Income

Description	Amount
Cash sales	125.95

	Amount
Total Income	125.95

Cost of Goods Sold

Description | Amount

(eg stock, inventory, materials sold to customers or used to manufacture goods sold to customers)

	Amount
Total Cost of Sales	

	Amount
Gross Profit	125.95

(Total Income less Cost of Sales)

Expenses

Description

(example - Advertising, Stationery, Postage, Fuel)

Description	Amount
Electricity	37.26

	Amount
Total Expenses	37.26

	Amount
Net Profit	88.69

(Gross Profit less Expenses)

179

Chapter 9: Accounting Systems:

Principles

The first eight chapters of this book have explored the fundamentals of bookkeeping. These chapters have discussed the two types of bookkeeping systems – single-entry and double-entry; the two types of accounting methods – cash and accrual; the accounting and bookkeeping cycle from collecting records of business transactions, to recording transactions in a journal, to posting them in a ledger, to creating financial statements at the end of the accounting and bookkeeping cycle. Clearly, every business may face a multitude of varying challenges on any given day, so it is not possible to foresee every possibility you may encounter in your efforts in professional bookkeeping. However, the previous chapters have mentioned one concern that deserves additional attention.

The main function of bookkeeping is to allow business owners to formulate an accurate assessment of their business's overall financial condition and performance. This chapter explores some of the ways well-designed financial statements can help business owners, investors, and financial regulators accurately assess the current state of financial health of any given business, as well as its potential for increased profitability and growth.

Figure 10: Free Image

Knowing How to Run Your Business

Running a business effectively requires a broad range of knowledge and access to resources. Perhaps most important, the business owner must understand the value of the goods and services his or her business will be providing, and how to produce and deliver high-quality products and services. Consider the vast array of products and services that are available in both local and global markets:

- Consumer retail businesses such as department stores
- Hotels and restaurants

- Automobile dealerships and repair services
- Grocery stores
- Hobbies and other specialized interests, such as camping and outdoor living; musical instrument sales and instruction; pet supply stores, etc.
- Real estate and investing firms
- Legal and other professional service firms
- Advertising, sales, and marketing
- Technology supplies and service

The list is virtually endless. Each sector of business requires extensive knowledge not only of the specifics of the types of goods and services a given area of business should be able to provide, but also more general business knowledge, including advertising; personnel management; lead generation; occupational safety and health; public relations; and much more.

But regardless of the specific nature and the day-to-day details of operating your business, all businesses share one common aspect: bookkeeping is an essential daily function. It is true that providing quality goods and services that answer a genuine need or desire will always be one of the key aspects of success in the professional world. However, even a business that offers the highest quality goods and services can suffer and fail financially if they do not employ effective financial management tools.

Gaining Knowledge of a Business Through Bookkeeping

The three main types of financial statements – the balance sheet; the income statement; and the cash flow statement – each provide unique opportunities for gaining knowledge about any given business's core functions, profitability, competitiveness, and potential of further growth. Furthermore, the reason these three types of reports have been identified as the standard for financial statements that comply with Generally Accept Accounting Principles (GAAP) is because each type of report allows for the assessment of a different aspect of the business's performance. Together, all three allow for complete knowledge of the business's operations.

Many people may be interested in analyzing financial performance records to gain knowledge of a business. For example, the following occupational groups routinely seek to know businesses through a deep understanding of their business operations:

- **Creditors**. Any financial services organization that issues business loans will ask questions to determine whether the company has the capacity to repay. Often, they will request cash flow statements, so they can determine whether a company exercises appropriate discipline in the regulation of its expenses and income.

- **Investors**. If you work for or own a company that issues shares or is managed by investment partners, these individuals will be interested in examining financial statements for evidence that the company will be able to continue paying dividends to existing investors, or whether the company may be an attractive opportunity for future investors.

- **Management**. The goal of business management is to ensure that the company maintains operational efficiency and profitability. While ensuring that the needs of personnel and facilities are addressed is a very important aspect of management, no management team can assess whether their efforts are successful without examining the financial statements at the end of each accounting cycle.

- **Financial regulators**. Publicly held companies are required to submit financial statements to the Securities and Exchange Commission (SEC) to ensure GAAP compliance. In addition, any business may be audited by the IRS, and financial statements will be the main source of information.

Those interested in gaining knowledge of any business may choose to focus on one type of report over another depending upon their concerns. Specifically, each of the three types of reports may offer the following types of insights:

- **Balance sheets**: These reports can help investors and regulators determine such factors as asset turnover, receivables turnover, debt-to-asset ratios, and debt-to-equity ratios. Thus, the balance sheet provides a means to gain knowledge of a company's essential value at a given point in time.

- **Income statements**: These reports help investors and regulators determine a given company's gross profit margin, net profit margin, ratio of tax efficiency, and interest coverage.

- **Cash flow statements**: These reports help investors and regulators assess a company's ability to generate cash-driven revenue by showing the relationship between cash and overall earnings before interest, taxes, depreciation, and amortization. Thus, simply because a company can report a net profit at the end of the year does not necessarily mean that they have been successful in selling goods and services – this report can help determine whether profitability resulted instead from non-operating activity, such as loans or investments.

Analyzing Financial Reports

This section examines the specific types of financial analysis, as well as an overview of processes commonly employed to gain knowledge of businesses by examining their financial records.

Essentially, there are two types of financial analysis:

- Horizontal and vertical analysis
- Ratio analysis

Horizontal and Vertical Analysis

This type of financial analysis is typically used to analyze the results of income statements.

First, horizontal analysis compares the performance of certain aspect of a business's financial performance over two or more accounting periods. A horizontal analysis of any business may compare the change from one year to the next of a single aspect of its balance sheet – for example, a company's gross profits from sales. This analysis of the year-over-year (YoY) change in any given line item of a financial statement uses a specific formula:

Percentage of Change= (Value of Period N)/(Value of Period N-1)-1.

For example, let's calculate the YoY change in gross profits between 2017 and 2016 for Company ABC:

- In 2017, the company generated $4,000 gross profit in sales.

- In 2016, gross profit from sales was $3,000.

- YoY change is calculated as follows:

    - Percentage of YoY change = ($4,000 / $3,000) – 1

    - Percentage of YoY change = 1.33 – 1

    - Percentage of YoY change = .33

    - YoY change = 33%

Next, vertical analysis compares the line items of any given financial report within one single year to understand the significance of the relationships among the various statistics for that reporting year. For this example, we will consider the income statement for Company ABC. In the following illustration, you can see on the left the breakdown of the company's income; on the right, you can see an analysis of those numbers that shows the percentage of each figure in relation to revenue:

Company ABC Income Statement		
	2018	**2018**
Revenue	500,000	100%
COGS	(300,200)	-64%
Gross Profit	**100,800**	**36%**
Depreciation	(500,000)	-10%
SG&A	(300,000)	-6%
Interest	(5,000)	-1%
Earnings before tax	**95,000**	**19%**
Tax	(22,500)	-5%
Net earnings	**72,500**	**15%**

Because this type of analysis compares statistical reporting data within one vertical column of figures, it is referred to as vertical analysis.

Ratio Analysis

Ratio analysis takes a different approach. Ratio analysis calculates the relative size or value of one statistic to another. This ratio is then used as a standard of comparison to determine how a company is performing – either in relation to a prior time period or to an industry standard. Generally, ration analysis should confirm expectations, but it can also indicate areas of concerns. There are several main categories of ratio analysis:

- Liquidity ratios measure the ability of a business to remain in operation by examining the following factors:
  - Cash coverage ratios comparing available cash to pay interest;
  - Current ratios measuring amount of liquid assets available to pay liabilities;
  - Quick ratios, which are the same as current ratios, except that they exclude inventory;
  - Liquidity index, which measures how long it will take to convert assets to cash.
- Activity ratios show how well a company is managing the use of its resources and include:

- o   Accounts payable turnover ratios
- o   Accounts receivable turnover ratios
- o   Fixed asset turnover ratio
- o   Inventory turnover ratio
- o   Sales to working capital ratio
- o   Working capital turnover ratio
- Leverage ratios measure the degree to which a company is relying on debt to maintain operations and includes the following:
  - o   Debt-to-equity ratio
  - o   Debt service coverage ratio
  - o   Fixed charge coverage ratio
- Profitability ratios measure the ability of a company to generate profit and include:
  - o   Break-even point ratio
  - o   Contribution margin ratio
  - o   Gross profit ratio
  - o   Margin of safety
  - o   Net profit ratio
  - o   Return on equity ratio
  - o   Return on net assets ratio
  - o   Return on operating assets ratio

Decision Making Through Effective Bookkeeping

Thus, there are two sides to effectively managing any type of business. Producing quality goods and services, selling them at competitive rates and prices, and ensuring that people are aware of your business are absolute essentials. Without these skills, no one would have any business to manage. It may be tempting to assume that you can make effective business decisions based exclusively on your expertise in your given field of professional work or your skill as a personnel manager. However, to make your business stand out and reach its full potential, you must harness the power of effective bookkeeping to gain insights into the ways your business operations can remain competitive.

The following six steps of the financial analysis process explain how a thorough understanding of the bookkeeping and accounting cycle can help you be a better business owner, or help you be a better bookkeeper for the business owners you serve:

1.   Analyze the economics of the industry in which you are working.

Although GAAP-compliant bookkeeping and accounting methods apply across all industry lines, each industry will have its own particular characteristics. What types of goods or services does your industry produce? What is the industry standard method of producing and distributing these goods and services? Identifying the costs involved in these methods is known as a "value chain analysis," and you will be at a competitive disadvantage until you have a thorough understanding of your industry.

2.   Establish a competitive strategy.

Consider the type of product or service your company offers. Is your product or service unique? What are your profit margins and access to other forms of capital? What about brand recognition? Have you assessed the demographic in which you will be offering goods and services? What strategy can you implement that will address all of these concerns?

3.   Examine the financial statements.

Now that you have identified a specific business objective and a plan for achieving that objective, you can approach an analysis of the company's financial statements form an educated perspective. For each of the three types of reports, consider the following:

- Balance sheet: Does the company have sufficient assets to continue operating?

- Income statement: How successful is the company at generating revenue from sales of goods and services?

- Cash flow statement: Does the company exercise good judgment in managing its funds?

4. Conduct a thorough financial analysis.

Using the techniques of horizontal, vertical, and ratio analysis discussed earlier in this chapter, conduct a complete analysis of the company's performance. Focus specifically on areas you may have identified in the previous steps as needing improvement. How profitable is the company? Has performance been improving or declining? What does a financial analysis tell you about the areas that require greater attention?

5. Make recommendations

As the company's bookkeeper, you are in a unique position to contribute to a discussion of the direction of the company's direction for future growth and investment. Although market research and an assessment of the quality of the goods and services your company provides is a necessary part of this conversation, the hard date derived from a disciplined analysis of well-maintained and reliable accounting and bookkeeping records can provide invaluable insight.

6.   Issue an official valuation of the company.

Especially if you are part of a publicly traded company, an annual statement that places a total value on the company can be the most important driver of success. If you are required to submit reports to the SEC, it is imperative that you show documentation of the reliability of your calculations. If you are a smaller, privately held company, a disciplined valuation can still allow you to benefit by appearing to be a more attractive investment to lenders, clients, and customers.

Chapter 10: QuickBooks

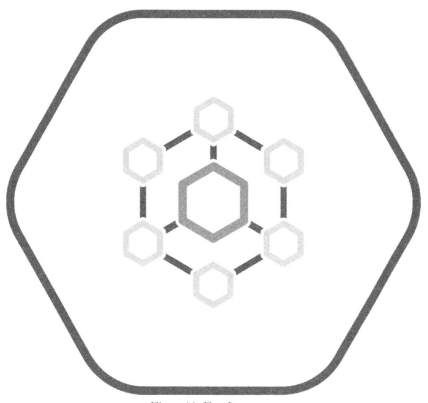

Figure 11: Free Image

A basic search using an internet search engine and the search term, "bookkeeping software," returns millions of results. There are over well over 20 recognized, well-known software applications that help business owners with a variety of bookkeeping and software tasks. Some of these services are available as software downloads and function as offline desktop applications that simply automate many bookkeeping and accounting chores. Others are available for purchases in office supply stores and offer similar features. Still others are designed as web-based applications that require an internet connection so that data can be stored in an off-site server. Web-based bookkeeping applications have become the most prominent type of bookkeeping software. Most of them require users to pay a monthly fee – usually about $10 per month for the most basic level of service. Among these types of automated bookkeeping software applications, some companies offer considerably more expensive versions that include the services of a human bookkeeping and accounting staff employed by the software company.

By far the most well-known of all these automated bookkeeping applications is QuickBooks, which was developed by Intuit Corporation. QuickBooks routinely receives the highest ratings of all major bookkeeping and accounting software applications and is generally considered the standard for the industry. Intuit, along with many independent, third-party companies have made available on the internet a vast selection of training videos and tutorials to help business owners learn how to navigate this powerful bookkeeping software. This chapter will cover some of the more basic functions to help you understand how software can help you make the bookkeeping process more efficient and reliable.

What Is QuickBooks? Why Should I Use It?

QuickBooks is accounting software designed to serve the needs of small- and medium-sized businesses. QuickBooks offers both desktop accounting applications and cloud- and web-based applications. QuickBooks is adaptable to most accounting and bookkeeping environments and includes many features, such as accepting and processing of payment for business services; payment and management of bills; customer and client invoicing; and employee payroll processing.

Although initial versions of the software did not accommodate double-entry accounting methods, it became very popular very quickly with many small business owners who had no formal training in bookkeeping and accounting. Subsequent updates have allowed QuickBooks to address many of the shortcomings of its earlier releases.

Beginning in 2000, QuickBooks was available in two versions – Basic and Pro. In 2002, an Enterprise version was released for medium-sized businesses. As of 2003, QuickBooks has released customized versions with specific functions and workflows designed specifically to meet the needs of differing types of businesses, such as manufacturing, wholesale, professional service firms, retailers, and non-profit organizations. There is even a version specifically designed for professional accountants that is capable of addressing all GAAP-required functions, such as creating audit trails and generating highly detailed professional financial statements. Over 50,000 accounting firms are members of the QuickBooks ProAdvisor program, and as of 2008, almost 95% of the bookkeeping software market was dominated by QuickBooks. The most recent versions of QuickBooks included updates that enable batch transactions, bill tracking, automated reports, smart search, and improved report filters.

QuickBooks Online

Figure 12: Free Image

QuickBooks offers an online web-based service called QuickBooks Online. To use this service, the user must register and pay a monthly fee. QuickBooks Online provides access to software functions through the internet instead of directly on the user's computer.

QuickBooks Online is a different product than the original QuickBooks accounting software. The online version includes ongoing updates and patches, but also includes pop-ads for upgrade services. Like the desktop application, QuickBooks Online is also the industry leader among web-based accounting applications. However, there are many products and services that offer greater competition to QuickBooks Online than to the desktop version.

QuickBooks Online is accessible through all major browsers and through all major devices, including mobile devices using Android or iOS operating systems. QuickBooks Online received a major redesign in 2013 and now allows for customization and integration with other third-party software and the proprietary applications of financial services companies such as banks and payroll management companies.

Setting Up a QuickBooks Inventory

There are thousands of tutorials and videos available online on the Intuit website as well as many third-party education and training sites. These videos and tutorials range from one-session how-to lessons about a specific function in QuickBooks all the way to complete training and certification courses designed for use by human resources departments. There are far too many possible bookkeeping scenarios involving far too much complexity to provide complete, detailed illustrations in this book. However, we have included below a brief overview of how to set up an inventory using QuickBooks to illustrate the usefulness of this bookkeeping and accounting software.

Note: The Inventory function described in this section is only available using a Plus-level subscription to QuickBooks Online.

1.   **Sales** settings

   a.   Click on the **Gear** icon in the upper right corner of the **Home Page**.

   b.   Select **Accounts and Settings** from the dropdown menu.

   The **Accounts and Settings** page will appear on the screen.

   c.   From the **Accounts and Settings** page, click Sales at the left of the screen.

   d.   In the **Sales** window confirm that "**Track quantity and price/rate**" and "**Track inventory quantity on hand**" are set to **On**.

   e.   Click the "x" in the upper-right corner to close the window.

2.   **Products and Services** settings

   a.   Click on the **Gear** icon in the upper right corner of the **Home Page**.

   b.   Select **Products and Services** from the drop-down menu.

The **Products and Services** page will appear on the screen.

c.   Create product categories:

    i.   Select **Manage Categories** in the upper-left corner.

         The **Product Categories** page will appear.

    ii.   Click **New Category** in the upper-left corner.

    iii.   Enter a name for the category in the **Name** field.

    iv.   Click **Save**.

d.   Create sub-categories.

    i.   Select **Manage Categories** in the upper-left corner.

         The **Product Categories** page will appear.

    ii.   Click **New Category** in the upper-left corner.

    iii.   Enter a name for the sub-category in the **Name** field.

    iv.   Check the "**Is a sub-category**" box beneath the **Name** field.

v.   Select the parent category from the drop-down menu beneath the **Name** field.

vi.   Click **Save**.

e.   Add products manually

i.   From the **Products and Services** page, click **New**.

ii.   Select an **Inventory Item**.

The item detail pane will appear.

iii.   Add as many details about the item as you would like, such as name, number, quantity, etc. There is also a space to add a picture.

iv.   Click **Save**.

f.   Alternatively, you can import product lists from an Excel spreadsheet.

i.   Form the **Products and Services** page, click the arrow next to **New**.

ii.   Click **Import**.

iii.   Click **Download a Sample File** to see how to format your existing spreadsheet.

iv.   After you have formatted your spreadsheet, click **Browse**.

v.   Select the appropriate file from your computer and follow the on-screen instructions.

g.   Create a purchase order to buy inventory.

i.   From the **Home Page,** click the **Plus Sign**.

ii.   Click **Purchase Order**.

A purchase order form will appear.

iii.   Complete the details in the **Purchase Order** form.

iv.   Click **Save and send**.

The purchase order will be sent to your supplier.

h.   Create a bill for the purchase order

i.   From the **Home Page**, choose **Transactions** on the left menu.

ii.   Choose **Expenses**.

iii.   Select the purchase order you created in (i).

iv.   Click the arrow to the right of the **Send** button.

A drop-down menu appears.

v.   Click **Copy to bill.**

A bill will be generated for the purchase order.

vi.   Check the details.

vii.   Click **Save and send**.

i.   Generate an invoice for customer sales.

i.   From the **Home Page,** click the **Plus Sign.**

ii.   Click **Invoice**.

An invoice form will appear.

iii.   Complete the details.

iv.   Click **Save and Send**.

Inventory quantities will be automatically adjusted, and the customer will receive an invoice.

j.   Adjust Inventory manually.

i.   Click on the **Gear** icon in the upper right corner of the **Home Page.**

ii.   Select **Products and Services** from the drop-down menu.

The **Products and Services** page will appear on the screen.

iii.   Locate the item whose quantity you want to adjust.

iv.   Click on the arrow next to the **Edit** button.

v.   Click **Adjust Quantity.**

The **Inventory Quantity Adjustment** window appears.

vi.   Click in the **New QTY** box and enter the new quantity.

vii.   Click **Save and send**.

k.   View Inventory Reports.

      i.   From the **Home Page**, choose **Reports** on the left menu.

            The Reports page appears.

      ii.   Click **All Reports**.

            The **All Reports** page appears.

      iii.   Choose **Manage Products and Inventory**.

      iv.   The **Manage Products and Inventory** window appears.

      v.   Click **Sales by Product/Service Summary**. (You may also view the **Inventory Valuation Summary** or any of the other available reports.)

            The **Sales by Product/Service Summary** report appears.

Chapter 11: Adapting the Basics

of Bookkeeping to Different

Businesses

By now, you have absorbed the basic fundamentals of bookkeeping and accounting; their importance to running a business successfully; and the many options available to all business owners interested in streamlining their operations. This chapter will address one final concern. As the examples in the previous chapters have illustrated, the size, complexity, and type of any given business is one of the most important considerations when deciding which type of bookkeeping and accounting methods are most appropriate. So, in this chapter, we will explore specifically how bookkeeping methods can be adapted to ensure the needs and demands of any business are best served. Specifically, this chapter explores how the bookkeeping priorities may differ among three types of businesses:

- retail sales and/or restaurants;
- real estate companies;
- personal and/or professional service companies.

Retail and Restaurants

For most of us, a business is a place where we go to do our shopping, pay for essential services, or spend time in leisure activities. We have all grown comfortable with the idea of huge multinational corporations with billion-dollar budgets and global offices equipped with satellite communication. Many of us are employed by such organizations, and if you are reading this book, you may work in the bookkeeping and accounting department of large corporations. On the other hand, the bookkeeping needs of smaller, local businesses are vastly different than the concerns of global competition faced by Wall Street corporations. Let's examine how a smaller retail business or restaurant can optimize its bookkeeping:

Inventory

If you operate a retail business, your inventory is the most important asset. In fact, of all your investments, inventory may represent the largest percentage. As a result, your inventory tracking system should reflect the importance of this aspect of your business. Here's what your bookkeeping records should record:

- Daily changes to inventory quantities resulting from shipments received and customer sales.

- Quantities and costs of all shipments received, and all products sold.

- Regular adjustments to account for lost, stolen, or damaged items.

If you are keeping the books for a restaurant, you should also keep track of the following concerns:

- Changes in daily food inventory, including dates and lists of every item purchased.

- Daily food sales, including the number of meals served during each meal period of the day.

- Location where meals were served.

- Revenues associated with meal sales.

- Beverage sales, including types of beverages, quantities, times sold, and revenue earned.

Income

All sources of income should be recorded. Obviously, in retail sales, sales should be the main source of revenue, and your records should be as detailed as possible. But there are other sources of income that should be recorded as well, such as after-sale service fees. You will also want to set up a system to conduct regular audits of point-of-sale machinery to ensure there are no inaccuracies.

If you are keeping books for a restaurant, you should also consider a system that allows each cash register to record individual sales, as well as cash transactions conducted by servers, including taxes, tips, and payments by credit card.

Expenses

Regardless of the type of retail business you run, you should automate as many payment expenses as you can, such as utilities, rent and lease payments, and any other regularly occurring payments. Expenses also include employees' wages and payroll taxes, so you should set up an entirely separate bookkeeping system to ensure compliance with all applicable laws. Make sure you also provide a space for insurance, marketing, administrative expenses, depreciation, loan payments, startup costs, and anticipated repairs and maintenance costs.

Accounts Payable and Receivable

Be sure to keep detailed records of all the money you owe and all the money that is owed to you. If you use automated bookkeeping software, set up reminders for loan payments, bills, and credit debts, as well as to guide collections activities for credit customers. These bookkeeping items are crucial to a small store or restaurant and managing your payables and receivables effectively can boost your credit rating and help you maintain a positive cash flow.

Retained Earnings

You're in business for a reason: to come out ahead financially. Make sure all of your bookkeeping and accounting is designed to help you find ways to save money, increase profitability and efficiency, and monitor the growth of your re-investment.

Real Estate

Like retail businesses and restaurants, real estate companies should have a system that records income and expenses. But real estate investment is an entirely different type of business venture that requires adaptations of the bookkeeping system:

- Inventory. For a real estate investor, the inventory is the prospective homes and buildings he or she may either sell or purchase for profit. These are not simple inventory items that need to be accounted for merely by tracking quantities and costs. The real estate investment business is complex, and your inventory is your main concern. Your bookkeeping system needs to be able to track the multitude of factors that are used to determine competitive market prices.

- Business metrics. As a real estate investor, your financial concerns extend beyond your own personal investment goals and the soundness of your company's finances. Having readily available data and analytics to help you understand the financial backgrounds of your clients, customers, and the real estate market generally will make the determination of whether your real estate investment firm is successful. Ensure your bookkeeping system can account for all of the following factors:
  - Job performance across your entire network.
  - Tax preparedness
  - Cash flow awareness
  - Credit score management

Personal and Professional Service Firms

Finally, professional service companies may have unique concerns because unlike retail stores, restaurants, and real estate firms, they are not selling any tangible items. Because this business model is radically different from retail consumer sales, the bookkeeping systems should be able to address a different set of concerns as well.

To begin, professional service firms will have less of a concern about initiating inventory records. Professional service firms may offer a wide variety of professional services:

- Legal services
- Medical services
- Counseling service
- Tax filing services
- Consulting in a variety of areas.

Because of the potential for malpractice and other types of litigation, the success of a professional service firm may be more heavily dependent on the firm's sound financial foundation. Here are some of the considerations commonly addressed by the accounting systems of professional service firms:

- monthly costs like billable hours, travel, and marketing.
- client billing systems that incorporate medical insurance billing or other types of compensation.
- cash flow statements and commission tracking reports to determine whether your practice is profitable.

- continuing education, training, certification, and accreditation.

Every business will have unique challenges and concerns. However, bookkeeping and accounting methods and systems have been firmly established across all areas of business. No matter how big or small, or how simple or complex your business model, a well-designed bookkeeping and accounting system can help you operate more efficiently, profitably, and effectively.

Chapter 12: Glossary

Common Terms Used in Bookkeeping and Accounting

Account: A space in a ledger reserved for recording all the transactions of a specific type. For example, all sales transactions will be recorded in the Sales account.

Accounting: the practice of entering bookkeeping records into a ledger and producing financial statements.

Accounting Equation: the accounting equation is Assets = Liabilities + Owners' Equity. It is used to ensure that all records in a double-entry accounting system are balanced.

Accountant: the person responsible for processing and evaluating bookkeeping records. Sometimes used interchangeably with "bookkeeper."

Accounts Payable (A/P): all invoices and other expanse that a business has not yet paid.

Accounts Receivable (A/R): all revenue owed to a company that has not yet been paid.

Accrual Accounting: an accounting method in which income and expenses are recognized at the time they are incurred, instead of at the time they are paid.

Assets: all items of value that a company owns.

Bad Debts: sales invoices that have not been paid by customers, and that the company has written off as an expense.

Balance Sheet: one of three reports that comprise financial statements. The balance sheet provides information about a company's value by showing its assets, liabilities, and equity at a given point in time. The other two reports are the income statement and the cash flow statement.

Billing: the practice of sending invoices to clients and customers for goods sold or services rendered.

Bookkeeper: a person trained and experienced in recording all the daily transactions of a business in journals and ledgers. Sometimes used interchangeably with "accountant."

Bookkeeping: the professional practice of recording business transactions in journals and ledgers according to Generally Accepted Accounting Principles (GAAP).

Bookkeeping Cycle: a complete cycle of recording transactions before the records are transferred to the ledger and balanced. Usually a bookkeeping cycle is one month.

Budget: a fixed sum of money within which a household or business must function.

Capital: generally, funds or other forms of assets invested into a business to enable operations.

Cash Accounting: a method of accounting in which income and expenses are recorded when they are paid, instead of when they are incurred.

Cash Book: the main record of financial transactions for a business.

Cash Flow: the movement or "flow" of cash through a business. A cash flow statement can show how the business owner manages the money the business generates through operations.

Chart of Accounts: a list of all accounts contained in a company's ledger. The main account categories are assets, Liabilities, Equity, Revenue, Cost of Goods Sold, and Expenses. Each category may contain several accounts that record specific types of transactions.

Closing Balance: the final balance on a bank statement or cash book register at the end of a business day or bookkeeping cycle.

Coding: the practice of assigning transaction amounts to accounts in the chart of accounts.

Contra: contra accounts allow bookkeepers to counterbalance an entry into a ledger account. The Allowance for Bad Debts account is a contra account to the Sales Revenue account.

Cost of Goods Sold: the amount of money a company pays for items they purchase wholesale and then sale at retail for a profit. This can also refer to the costs of raw materials to manufacture products for resale.

Credit: bookkeeping entries that are entered on the right side of a double-entry bookkeeping ledger. Credits increase the value of income, liability, and equity accounts and decrease the value of asset and expense accounts.

Credit Note: a receipt for money refunded to a customer who was overcharged or who returned an item.

Creditor: a person or business who lends money or extends credit.

Data: information stored in journals and ledgers.

Debit: bookkeeping entries that are entered on the left side of a double-entry bookkeeping ledger. Debits decrease the value of income, liability, and equity accounts and increase the value of asset and expense accounts.

Debtor: a person or business who borrows money.

Deductible: a purchase that can be claimed as a business expense.

Deposit: money paid into a bank account.

Deposit Slip: a receipt showing the date amount of a deposit.

Depreciation: the amount of value an asset loses due to wear and tear.

Description: the section of a financial transaction record that provides information about the customer and the item purchased.

Docket: a document that provides information about a shipment of items purchased.

Double-Entry: double-entry bookkeeping requires two entries for every transaction – a debit entry and a credit entry. Debit entries must always equal credit entries for every transaction.

Drawings: the owners' salary.

End of Month: the process that occurs each month when the bookkeeper completes the bookkeeping cycle.

Entry/Entries: refers to all recorded financial transactions.

Equity: the difference between a company's assets and its liabilities.

Expense: purchases made to support a company's operations.

Financial Statements: reports of financial activities that allow businesses, investors, and regulators to determine the financial health of a company. They include the balance sheet, income statement, and the cash flow statement.

Fiscal Year: twelve consecutive months that constitute an entire accounting and bookkeeping cycle. A fiscal year can begin in any calendar month.

Funds: all of the money involved in all of a business's transactions.

Gross Profit: total business income less the cost of goods sold.

Income: money earned by a business through sales of goods and services.

Inventory: all the items that a company keeps on its premises available for sale.

Invoice: a document that shows the details of a purchase, including the goods or services purchased, the date, and the amount owed.

Journal: a chronological record of daily business transactions.

Ledger: a permanent record of daily business transactions organized by account type. The information in the ledger is taken from the journal.

Liability: debts that accompany owes.

Loan: a sum of money extended to a company or person that must be repaid, usually with interest.

Loss: Loss occurs when expenses are greater than income. The opposite of profit.

Net Profit: the result of subtracting the cost of expenses from gross profit.

Nil: a balance of zero.

Opening Balance: the balance of a financial account on the first day of a financial period.

Payable: a bill that is due to be paid by a business to a customer that has not yet been paid.

Payroll: the financial account from which funds are distributed to employees.

Petty Cash: a financial account that consists of a small amount of physical cash, so businesses can make minor purchases.

Profit: the difference between income and expenses.

Purchase: buying goods or services.

Quote: an estimate of the cost of goods or services.

Receipt: a document issued by a business to a customer showing the details of a sale of goods or services.

Receivable: accounts that are due to be paid to a business that have not yet been paid by the customer.

Reconcile: matching the calculations or balances from one document to another, as when someone reconciles their checkbook balance with their bank statement.

Recurring: a transaction that takes place repeatedly, at a regular time interval, such as a monthly utility bill.

Refund: money that is given back to the customer or a business after a purchase as a result of a dispute, an overpayment, or some other reason.

Reimburse: payment in return for some type of loss

Salary: a fixed amount of money paid to an employee for an agreed period of employment.

Sales: money received for goods or service purchased by customers.

Single-Entry: a bookkeeping method in which all financial transactions are only listed once.

Software: computer programs like QuickBooks that automate certain clerical or other tasks.

Statement: reports that display financial information, such as bank statements, or financial statements).

Transaction: a transfer of funds as a result of a sale or purchase.

Transfer: movement of funds from one account to another, usually for accounting purposes.

Undeposited Funds: an asset account showing funds that have not yet been deposited into the bank.

Unpresented: checks that have been written, sent, and received, but not yet deposited.

Withdrawal: money taken out of a financial account.

Write-Off: an amount of money owed that will not be paid.

Year-End: the financial accounting and bookkeeping activities that occur at the end of a fiscal year.

Resources

6 Steps to an Effective Financial Statement Analysis. (n.d.). Retrieved from https://www.afponline.org/ideas-inspiration/topics/articles/Details/6-steps-to-an-effective-financial-statement-analysis.

A guide to retail accounting. (n.d.). Retrieved from https://www.business.com/articles/jill-bowers-retail-accounting/

A Relatively Painless Guide to Double-Entry Accounting: Bench Accounting. (n.d.). Retrieved from https://bench.co/blog/accounting/double-entry-accounting

About Publication 583, Starting a Business and Keeping Records. (n.d.). Retrieved from https://www.irs.gov/forms-pubs/about-publication-583.

Account Types. (n.d.). Retrieved from https://www.principlesofaccounting.com/account-types/.

Accounting Basics: Debits and Credits. (2019, September 11). Retrieved from https://www.patriotsoftware.com/accounting/training/blog/debits-and-credits/.

Accounting for Contractors: Software, Billing & Taxes. (2016, October 19). Retrieved from https://www.homeadvisor.com/r/new-contractor-accounting-basics.

Accounts, Debits, and Credits. (n.d.). Retrieved from https://www.principlesofaccounting.com/chapter-2/accounts-debits-and-credits/.

Adamson-Pickett, J. (2019, October 11). Small Business Bookkeeping Basics. Retrieved from https://www.business.org/finance/accounting/small-business-bookkeeping-basics.

Albarado, L. M., Norman, A., Afzaal, M., Payne, P., Shelton, C., & Khlynovskiy, R. (2019, March 6). 39 Free QuickBooks Online Tutorials: Learn QuickBooks Fast. Retrieved from https://fitsmallbusiness.com/free-quickbooks-online-tutorials/.

Analysis of Financial Statements - Free Financial Analysis Guide. (n.d.). Retrieved from https://corporatefinanceinstitute.com/resources/knowledge/finance/analysis-of-financial-statements/.

Articles. (n.d.). Retrieved from https://www.afponline.org/ideas-inspiration/topics/articles/Details/6-steps-to-an-effective-financial-statement-analysis.

Balance Sheet Template for Excel. (n.d.). Retrieved from https://www.vertex42.com/ExcelTemplates/cash-flow-statement.html.

Beginners Guide to Financial Statement. (2007, February 5). Retrieved from https://www.sec.gov/reportspubs/investor-publications/investorpubsbegfinstmtguidehtm.html.

Bhosale, T., & *, N. (2019, October 9). General Journal vs General Ledger: Top 5 Differences (with Infographics). Retrieved from https://www.wallstreetmojo.com/general-journal-vs-general-ledger/.

Bookkeeping, S. L. C. (n.d.). Personal Tax Services. Retrieved from https://www.slcbookkeeping.com/personal-tax-services.

Bookkeeping - Double-Entry, Debits and Credits: AccountingCoach. (n.d.). Retrieved from https://www.accountingcoach.com/bookkeeping/explanation/3.

Bookkeeping Basics - Steps for Business Startups. (n.d.). Retrieved from https://www.beginner-bookkeeping.com/bookkeeping-basics.html.

Bookkeeping Basics: A How-To Guide for Small Business Owners: Bench Accounting. (n.d.). Retrieved from https://bench.co/bookkeeping-basics/.

Bookkeeping for Business: What You Need to Know. (n.d.). Retrieved from https://www.fundera.com/business-accounting/small-business-bookkeeping.

Bookkeeping Terms and Basic Accounting Definitions. (n.d.). Retrieved from https://www.beginner-bookkeeping.com/bookkeeping-terms.html.

Botkeeper. (n.d.). Bookkeeping for Professional Services. Retrieved from https://www.botkeeper.com/bookkeeping-for-professional-services.

Bragg, S. (2018, November 28). Financial statements. Retrieved from https://www.accountingtools.com/articles/2017/5/10/financial-statements.

Bragg, S. (2019, August 17). Debits and credits. Retrieved from https://www.accountingtools.com/articles/2017/5/17/debits-and-credits.

Bragg, S. (2019, April 10). The difference between a journal and a ledger. Retrieved from https://www.accountingtools.com/articles/what-is-the-difference-between-a-journal-and-a-ledger.html.

Bragg, S. (2019, March 20). Financial statement analysis. Retrieved from https://www.accountingtools.com/articles/2017/5/14/financial-statement-analysis.

Cash Basis Accounting vs. Accrual Accounting: Bench Accounting. (n.d.). Retrieved from https://bench.co/blog/accounting/cash-vs-accrual-accounting/.

Cash Flow Statement Template for Excel. (n.d.). Retrieved from https://www.vertex42.com/ExcelTemplates/cash-flow-statement.html.

Chart of accounts. (2019, September 27). Retrieved from https://en.wikipedia.org/wiki/Chart_of_accounts.

Chen, J. (2019, April 25). Accounting Method. Retrieved from https://www.investopedia.com/terms/a/accountingmethod.asp.

Chou, L. (2019, June 26). Guide to Financial Statement Analysis for Beginners. Retrieved from https://towardsdatascience.com/guide-to-financial-statement-analysis-for-beginners-835d551b8e29.

Chughtai, B., Norman, A., Julia, Robinson, Parker, J., Shelton, C., & Debitoor, W. (2019, June 11). Small Business Bookkeeping, Accounting & Tax Guide. Retrieved from https://fitsmallbusiness.com/small-business-bookkeeping-accounting-the-ultimate-guide/.

Closing the Books. (n.d.). Retrieved from https://www.accountingtools.com/closing-the-books.

Debits and credits. (2019, October 3). Retrieved from https://en.wikipedia.org/wiki/Debits_and_credits.

Debits and Credits: A Simple, Visual Guide: Bench Accounting. (n.d.). Retrieved from https://bench.co/blog/bookkeeping/debits-credits/.

Debits and Credits: Explanation: AccountingCoach. (n.d.). Retrieved from https://www.accountingcoach.com/debits-and-credits/explanation.

Decker, F. (2019, April 5). How to Keep Accounting Records for a Small Restaurant. Retrieved from https://smallbusiness.chron.com/keep-accounting-records-small-restaurant-56253.html.

Double Entry Accounting Principles vs. Single Entry, Examples. (2019, September 11). Retrieved from https://www.business-case-analysis.com/double-entry-system.html.

Double Entry Bookkeeping in 7 Steps. (n.d.). Retrieved from https://www.beginner-bookkeeping.com/double-entry-bookkeeping.html.

Edunote.info@gmail.com. (2019, October 2). 7 Different Types of Journal Book. Retrieved from https://iedunote.com/types-of-accounting-journal.

Elmblad, S. (2019, May 19). What Is Double Entry Accounting? Retrieved from https://www.thebalance.com/what-is-double-entry-accounting-1293675.

Esajian, P. (2019, September 5). Real Estate Bookkeeping 101. Retrieved from https://www.fortunebuilders.com/real-estate-bookkeeping-managing-finances/.

Financial Accounting. (n.d.). Retrieved from https://courses.lumenlearning.com/sac-finaccounting/chapter/assets-liabilities-and-owners-equity/.

Financial Accounting. (n.d.). Retrieved from https://courses.lumenlearning.com/sac-finaccounting/chapter/preparing-a-trial-balance/.

Financial Accounting. (n.d.). Retrieved from https://courses.lumenlearning.com/sac-finaccounting/chapter/financial-statements/.

Financial statement. (2019, October 6). Retrieved from https://en.wikipedia.org/wiki/Financial_statement.

Financial statement analysis. (2019, August 16). Retrieved from https://en.wikipedia.org/wiki/Financial_statement_analysis.

Financial Statement Preparation: Example: Explanation of Steps. (n.d.). Retrieved from https://www.myaccountingcourse.com/accounting-cycle/financial-statement-preparation.

Financial Statements. (-1, November 30). Retrieved from https://www.inc.com/encyclopedia/financial-statements.html.

Free QuickBooks Tutorials - Learn How To Use QuickBooks. (2016, May 25). Retrieved from https://quickbookstraining.com/tutorials/.

FreshBooks. (n.d.). What is a Ledger in Accounting? Is There a Difference with a Journal and a Ledger? Retrieved from https://www.freshbooks.com/hub/accounting/what-is-a-ledger.

FreshBooks. (n.d.). How to Close the Books: 8 Steps for Small Business Owners. Retrieved from https://www.freshbooks.com/hub/accounting/closing-books.

Good bookkeeping: how to record receipts of transactions. (n.d.). Retrieved from https://www.ionos.com/startupguide/grow-your-business/good-bookkeeping-how-to-record-receipts-of-transactions/.

Grigg, B. A. (2019, October 8). Best Accounting Methods for Small Business: Fundera. Retrieved from https://www.fundera.com/blog/accounting-methods-for-small-business.

How to organize business receipts and paperwork. (2018, November 16). Retrieved from https://amynorthardcpa.com/organize-business-receipts-paperwork/.

Hyre, J., & Conflitti, J. (n.d.). Bookkeeping for Real Estate Investors: RWN Learning Center. Retrieved from https://www.realwealthnetwork.com/topics/bookkeeping/.

Income Statement Template for Excel. (n.d.). Retrieved from https://www.vertex42.com/ExcelTemplates/cash-flow-statement.html.

Ingram, D. (2016, October 26). How to Do Bookkeeping for a Store. Retrieved from https://smallbusiness.chron.com/bookkeeping-store-69569.html.

Investopedia. (2019, September 13). The Difference Between a General Ledger and a General Journal. Retrieved from https://www.investopedia.com/ask/answers/030915/whats-difference-between-general-ledger-and-general-journal.asp.

Irby, L. T. (2019, May 14). The 8 Best Receipt Scanners and Trackers of 2019. Retrieved from https://www.thebalancesmb.com/best-receipt-scanners-and-trackers-4172461.

Kehrer, D. (2019, March 21). The 10 Bookkeeping Basics You Can't Ignore. Retrieved from https://www.score.org/resource/10-bookkeeping-basics-you-cant-ignore.

Kenton, W. (2019, September 12). Financial Statement Analysis. Retrieved from https://www.investopedia.com/terms/f/financial-statement-analysis.asp.

Learn the Basics of Closing Your Books. (n.d.). Retrieved from https://www.bizfilings.com/toolkit/research-topics/finance/basic-accounting/learn-the-basics-of-closing-your-books.

Ledger, General Ledger Role in Accounting Defined and Explained. (2019, September 11). Retrieved from https://www.business-case-analysis.com/ledger.html.

Leonard, K. (2019, March 1). The Differences Between Debit & Credit in Accounting. Retrieved from https://smallbusiness.chron.com/differences-between-debit-credit-accounting-4063.html.

Lewis, M. R. (2019, March 29). How to Understand Debits and Credits. Retrieved from https://m.wikihow.com/Understand-Debits-and-Credits.

Marshall, D. (n.d.). Retrieved from http://www.dwmbeancounter.com/bookkeeping-systems.html.

Murphy, C. B. (2019, October 8). How to Interpret Financial Statements. Retrieved from https://www.investopedia.com/terms/f/financial-statements.asp.

Murray, J. (2019, January 25). A Business Guide to Deducting Legal and Professional Fees. Retrieved from https://www.thebalancesmb.com/deducting-legal-and-professional-fees-for-business-398955.

Nikolakopulos, A. (2017, November 21). Types of Bookkeeping. Retrieved from https://smallbusiness.chron.com/types-bookkeeping-48070.html.

Orange County Trusted Bookkeeper. (n.d.). Retrieved from https://ohanacpb.com/personal-bookkeeping/.

Outsource Services Home. (n.d.). Retrieved from https://www.outsource2india.com/financial/articles/book keeping-systems.asp.

Over 75 FREE QuickBooks Online training tutorials and videos. (n.d.). Retrieved from https://5minutebookkeeping.com/quickbooks-online-tutorials/.

Padhy, B. K. (2019, September 24). Debit vs Credit in Accounting: Top 7 Differences You Must Know! Retrieved from https://www.wallstreetmojo.com/debit-vs-credit-in-accounting/.

Padhy, B. K. (2019, September 24). Journal vs Ledger: Top 9 Must Know Differences (Infographics). Retrieved from https://www.wallstreetmojo.com/journal-vs-ledger/.

Peacock, L. (n.d.). Prevent Tax Troubles by Getting Organized in 2018. Retrieved from https://www.waveapps.com/blog/start-organizing-your-next-years-filing-now.

Peavler, R. (2019, May 4). The Business Owner's Guide to Accounting and Bookkeeping. Retrieved from https://www.thebalancesmb.com/bookkeeping-101-a-beginning-tutorial-392961.

Peavler, R. (2019, July 4). Tips and Guidance for Creating a General Ledger for Your Business. Retrieved from https://www.thebalancesmb.com/constructing-the-general-ledger-for-your-small-business-392998.

Peavler, R. (2019, July 12). You Need to Prepare These Financial Statements at the Cycle's End. Retrieved from https://www.thebalancesmb.com/prepare-the-financial-statements-393008.

Peavler, R. (2019, August 27). Use Horizontal and Vertical Analysis to Determine Financial Performance. Retrieved from https://www.thebalancesmb.com/how-do-you-do-financial-statement-analysis-393235.

Personal & Professional Services. (n.d.). Retrieved from https://rothcocpa.com/industries/personal-professional-services/.

Preparation of Trial Balance: Steps in the Preparation of Trial Balance. (2019, September 4). Retrieved from https://www.toppr.com/guides/principles-and-practice-of-accounting/trial-balance/preparation-of-trial-balance/.

Preparing a Trial Balance for Your Business. (n.d.). Retrieved from https://www.dummies.com/business/accounting/preparing-a-trial-balance-for-your-business/.

Qadeem, A. (2016, June 19). T-Accounts Ledger: Format: Examples. Retrieved from http://www.accountingsheet.com/accounting-cycle/t-accounts/.

QuickBooks. (2019, September 4). Retrieved from https://en.wikipedia.org/wiki/QuickBooks.

QuickBooks Tutorials - Learn How To Use QuickBooks. (n.d.). Retrieved from https://quickbooks.intuit.com/tutorials/.

Rampton, J. (2019, June 24). Complete Guide to Double-Entry Bookkeeping. Retrieved from https://quickbooks.intuit.com/global/resources/bookkeeping/complete-guide-to-double-entry-bookkeeping/.

REIbooks – Bookkeeping Solutions for Real Estate Investors. (n.d.). Retrieved from https://reibooksonline.com/.

Restaurant Accounting 101: How to Manage Your Bookkeeping. (n.d.). Retrieved from https://www.touchbistro.com/blog/restaurant-accounting-101-how-to-manage-your-bookkeeping.

Richards-Gustafson, F. (2017, November 21). How to Open a New Restaurant With Bookkeeping. Retrieved from https://smallbusiness.chron.com/open-new-restaurant-bookkeeping-26151.html.

Roberge, M. (n.d.). Restaurant Bookkeeping 101 - 5 Step Simple Guide. Retrieved from https://www.slcbookkeeping.com/blog/restaurant-bookkeeping-simple-5-step-guide.

Rosenberg, E. (2019, May 24). The 8 Best Accounting Apps for Independent Contractors in 2019. Retrieved from https://www.thebalance.com/best-accounting-apps-for-independent-contractors-4172220.

Singh, J. (2019, September 17). Financial Statement (Examples): Top 4 Types of Financial Statements. Retrieved from https://www.wallstreetmojo.com/financial-statements/.

Staff, I. (-1, November 30). Accounting Methods. Retrieved from https://www.inc.com/encyclopedia/accounting-methods.html.

Staff, M. F. (2016, March 20). What Is a Financial Statement? Retrieved from https://www.fool.com/knowledge-center/financial-statement.aspx.

Staff, W. (n.d.). A Complete Guide to Small Business Tax Season. Retrieved from https://www.waveapps.com/blog/the-complete-guide-to-small-business-tax-season.

Stafford, A. (n.d.). Should Real Estate Investors Be Using Accounting Software? Retrieved from https://www.therealestatecpa.com/blog/bookkeeping-for-real-estate-investors-should-you-be-using-accounting-software.

Dept. of the Treasury, Internal Revenue Service. Starting a business and keeping records, Starting a business and keeping records (1995). Washington, D.C.

Summary: Bookkeeping Basics. (n.d.). Retrieved from https://www.accountingtools.com/summary-bookkeeping-basics.

The General Ledger. (n.d.). Retrieved from https://www.principlesofaccounting.com/chapter-2/the-general-ledger/.

The Ultimate Guide to Real Estate Accounting. (n.d.). Retrieved from https://www.contactually.com/blog/real-estate-accounting.

Tuovila, A. (2019, September 30). Cash Book Definition. Retrieved from https://www.investopedia.com/terms/c/cash-book.asp.

Turner, B., Smith, S., Faircloth, M., & Sharkansky, M. (2019, June 29). The Investor's Guide to Excellent Real Estate Bookkeeping: Blog. Retrieved from https://www.biggerpockets.com/blog/2016-02-17-simple-guide-excellent-bookkeeping-real-estate-investing.

Types of Accounts in Accounting: Assets, Expenses, Liabilities, & More. (2019, July 2). Retrieved from https://www.patriotsoftware.com/accounting/training/blog/types-of-accounts-subaccounts-accounting/.

Understanding Accounting Methods. (n.d.). Retrieved from https://www.dummies.com/business/accounting/understanding-accounting-methods/.

WebstaurantStore. (2019, August 2). Restaurant Accounting Tips. Retrieved from https://www.webstaurantstore.com/article/134/restaurant-accounting-tips.html.

Weltman, B. (2019, June 29). Do I Need A Personal Accountant? Retrieved from https://www.investopedia.com/articles/personal-finance/040115/do-i-need-personal-accountant.asp.

What Are Assets, Liabilities, and Equity?: Bench Accounting. (n.d.). Retrieved from https://bench.co/blog/accounting/assets-liabilities-equity/.

What are the Different Types of Ledgers? (n.d.).
Retrieved from
https://www.accountingcapital.com/books-and-accounts/different-types-of-ledgers

What is a Bookkeeping System? (n.d.). Retrieved from
https://www.topaccountingdegrees.org/faq/what-is-a-bookkeeping-system/.

What Is Double-Entry Accounting?: Complete Small
Business Guide. (2017, November 20). Retrieved from
https://www.patriotsoftware.com/accounting/training/blog/an-overview-of-double-entry-bookkeeping/.

What is financial statement? definition and meaning.
(n.d.). Retrieved from
http://www.businessdictionary.com/definition/financial-statement.html.

What is the difference between a general ledger and
general journal?: AccountingCoach. (n.d.). Retrieved
from https://www.accountingcoach.com/blog/general-ledger-general-journal.

What kind of records should I keep. (n.d.). Retrieved from **https://www.irs.gov/businesses/small-businesses-%20self-employed/what-kind-of-records-should-i-keep.**

BOOK 2

ACCOUNTING FOR BEGINNERS

A Simple and Updated Guide to Learning Basic Accounting Concepts and Principles Quickly and Easily, Including Financial Statements and Adjusting Entries for Small Businesses

Warren Piper Ruell

Please note the information contained within this document is for educational and entertainment purposes only. All effort has been executed to present accurate, up to date, reliable, complete information. No warranties of any kind are declared or implied. Readers acknowledge that the author is not engaging in the rendering of legal, financial, medical or professional advice. The content within this book has been derived from various sources. Please consult a licensed professional before attempting any techniques outlined in this book.

By reading this document, the reader agrees that under no circumstances is the author responsible for any losses, direct or indirect, that are incurred as a result of the use of information contained within this document, including, but not limited to, errors, omissions, or inaccuracies.

Description

This book provides an essential overview of the established principles and practices of the accounting profession.

The accounting profession is among the oldest of the world's occupations. Modern versions of accounting practices that represent global standards date back to medieval Europe and even earlier. The current age of rapid technological innovation and the seemingly endless news stories of financial scandals have brought the field of professional accounting to the forefront of the American conversation. Also, far from limiting opportunities in the field of professional accounting, technological advances and developments in global business and finance have made professional careers in accounting more relevant, more exciting, and more in-demand than ever.

Accounting for Beginners is written for the small business owner, the aspiring accountant professional, and the busy professional looking for a quick and handy reference of the major conventions that govern this exciting field. When you read *Accounting for Beginners* you will learn about accounting fundamentals, including:

· Definitions of accounting and how accounting differs from bookkeeping.

· Financial statements:

o The balance sheet

o The income statement

o The cash flow statement

· Double-entry accounting, including debits, credits, and how to record transactions in journals and ledgers.

· Cash accounting vs. accrual accounting.

Accounting for Beginners also covers some of the more technical aspects of accounting, such as:

· Depreciation of fixed assets.

· Amortization of intangible assets.

· Budgeting for operational activities and capital expenditures .

· Recording costs for inventory and Cost of Goods Sold.

Next, *Accounting for Beginners* discusses many of the important professional practice conventions and regulatory foundations that professional CPAs must understand before earning a license, including:

· Generally Accepted Accounting Principles (GAAP)

· Background information about regulatory agencies such as the SEC, the AICPA, the FASB, and the GASB.

· Differences between U.S. accounting standards and international standards.

Finally, *Accounting for Beginners* discusses some of the more pressing concerns that face many of today's most successful accounting professionals, such as:

· Important principles and conventions of professional accounting firms.

· Fraud and ethics.

· Current fields actively seeking qualified accountants.

Whether you are currently considering a major course of study, pondering a career change, or actively engaged as a mid-career professional, *Accounting for Beginners* will give you a thorough and comprehensive review of established practices, a detailed guide to many of the most fundamental account recording techniques, and an experienced critique of the most pressing concerns and challenges facing contemporary CPAs.

Introduction

Accounting for Beginners: A Simple and Updated Guide to Learning Basic Accounting Concepts and Principles Quickly and Easily, Including Financial Statements and Adjusting Entries for Small Businesses provides and overview of essential concepts and practices for the accounting professional. *Accounting for Beginners* is the companion volume to *Bookkeeping for Beginners: Learning the Essential Basics of Bookkeeping for Small Businesses with Simple and Effective Methods Step-by-Step (Including Comprehensive Accounting, Financial Statements, and QuickBooks).*

Accounting and bookkeeping are related practices. As a result, both books discuss some of the same practices. However, there are important and fundamental differences between the responsibilities and concerns of the professional accountant and those of the professional bookkeeper. Chapter 1 discusses these differences in greater detail, but suffice it to say that although accounting addresses concerns that require more education, training and a higher level of authority, the focus of the accountant in many respects is much narrower than that of the bookkeeper. Whereas *Bookkeeping for Beginners* addresses some of the concerns of the accountant as they relate to the practice of professional bookkeeping, *Accounting for Beginners* explores the responsibilities of the accountant in greater depth and detail. In addition to an expanded discussion of double-entry accounting, cash vs. accrual methods, and financial statements, *Accounting for Beginners* also explores many areas that were not covered in *Bookkeeping for Beginners*, such as:

- Depreciation and Amortization
- Budgeting
- Inventory
- Generally Accepted Accounting Principles
- Fraud and Ethics

We hope you find this book a useful and reliable resources for all your professional accounting needs. Please also refer to the companion volume, *Bookkeeping for Beginners,* for more comprehensive coverage of all the essential principles and practices used in professional bookkeeping and accounting.

Chapter 1: Accounting Fundamentals and Financial Statements

Figure 13: Free Image

Accounting is among the oldest of all the world's professions. The earliest known forms of accounting date back to ancient Mesopotamia and parallel early developments in writing, counting, and money. Double-entry and modern accounting date back to the early medieval period in the Middle East among Jewish communities located in Iraq and Iran. Although some credit the invention of double-entry accounting to the Goryeo dynasty, which reigned in Korea from 912 through 1392, most people attribute all contemporary accounting methods to an Italian friar by the name of Luca Pacioli. A contemporary of Leonardo DaVinci, Pacioli's publication, *Summa de arithmetica, geometria, proportioni et proportionalita*, contains one of the first published descriptions of the double-entry accounting system. His system is still the standard for all professional accounting everywhere in the world. Pacioli is known as the "Father of Accounting."

Accounting is a fundamental part of the machinery not only of business, but of all of human civilization. Historians use accounting records for researching and archiving purposes; governments use accounting to ensure accountability, and businesses use accounting to increase efficiency and profitability. The interdependence of accounting to all human endeavors necessarily results in a system that can be complex and challenging. Yet, at the same time, the purpose of accounting is to translate these complexities into understandable and useful bits of information. This chapter provides a provides a concrete definition of accounting, a comparison of accounting to bookkeeping, and an overview of the main products of the accounting profession: financial statements.

What is Accounting?

Accounting is the professional practice of measuring, processing, analyzing, understanding, and communicating financial data about business, corporations and other officially recognized legal entities that engage in business transactions. The purpose of accounting is to gain an understanding of the financial condition—including its profitability, net value, and potential for growth—and then communicating that information to a wide variety of interested parties. Furthermore, accounting uses established rules and practices to ensure that information is communicated using a universally accepted and understood language.

By assessing the value of a company's assets, its liabilities, the amount of money invested into it by its owners and other shareholders, an accountant can establish a dollar figure to answer the question, "How much is my business worth today?" By assessing the amount of money a company has earned over a given period of time and subtracting the amount of money the same company has spent during the same period of time, an accountant can determine not only whether a business is profitable, but how profitable. Finally, by assessing how a company generates revenue and how it uses those funds, an accountant can determine how well a company manages its resources and whether there is any potential for growth or sustained production.

These three aspects of a company's finances are summarized in their financial statements—the balance sheet, the income statement, and the cash flow statement. Producing financial statements is one of the primary responsibilities of the professional accountant. By analyzing these three aspects of a company's finances—its net worth, its profitability, and its liquidity—a skilled accountant can make many determinations about a company's strengths or weaknesses.

Well-documented financial statements, in turn, are the only acceptable way for a business to present a record of its activities to the public or to any other interested parties, such as financial regulators and potential investors. If a business wants to secure a loan for new developments, the bank will request its financial statements. If a business wants to secure funding by seeking out new investors, the investors will request financial statements. If a business is audited by a financial regulatory agency, the auditors will request financial statements.

It is true that to succeed, a business must be able to provide its core goods and services in a competitive environment. However, without a sound financial foundation, no business will be able to afford the resources and infrastructure necessary to continue to offer those goods and services in any environment, regardless of competition. Thus, accounting provides the necessary foundation and framework required for long-term success in any area of business.

How Is Accounting Different from Bookkeeping?

For the most part, bookkeeping and accounting are regarded as separate but related professions; however, in many regards, the responsibilities of the bookkeeper and the accountant overlap. If accounting is the professional practice of measuring, processing, analyzing, understanding and communicating financial data, bookkeeping is the professional practice of recording all of the daily business transactions of a business that provide the information accountants need to formulate that financial data.

Bookkeeping may be thought of as the starting point of the "accounting cycle." The accounting cycle officially has six steps:

1. Analyzing and recording transactions
2. Posting transactions to the ledger
3. Preparing a trial balance
4. Preparing adjusting entries
5. Preparing an adjusted trial balance
6. Preparing financial statements

Thus, before an accountant can begin the cycle of accounting during any given period of financial activity, the bookkeeper must present a record of all the business transactions for that period. Put differently, the bookkeeper's responsibilities begin and end at ensuring every transaction of a business is recorded in an official journal. Once the bookkeeper has accomplished this goal, the information is handed off to the accountant, who translates those transactions into financial statements that tell the story of the business's financial life. Bookkeeping is itself an important and valuable profession. However, the bookkeeping profession requires far fewer certifications than the accounting profession. Although many bookkeepers may be certified as accountants, many do not have any official qualifications or degrees. Often, the contributions of a professional bookkeeper may be valued more by the wide array of on-the-job experience with bookkeeping and recording systems in different types of environment than for any formal training in finance. It is possible to gain certification as a bookkeeper, but it is not legally required.

On the other hand, accounting requires extensive education and certification. Most accountants are either Certified Public Accountants, Certified Management Accountants, or Certified Internal Auditors. As these titles imply, each of these positions require the accountant to pass a certification test. Becoming an accountant requires a bachelor's degree in accounting or other approved field of study. In addition, accountants may need to complete an additional year of certification. In the United States, requirements may vary from state to state, but all states require passage of the Uniform Certified Public Accountant Examination, which is administered by the American Institute of Certified Public Accountants.

What Are Financial Statements?

Figure 14: Free Image

As stated in the previous sections, the primary responsibility of the accountant is to produce financial statements that illustrate various aspects of a company's financial condition. The accounting profession has established three major reports that together comprise a company's official "financial statements." These statements are:

- Balance sheet
- Income statement
- Cash flow statement

Each of these statements focuses on a particular aspect of a company's financial picture. Specifically, the balance sheet illustrates how much a company is worth at a specific point in time, the income statement indicates how much money a company earned over a specified period of time, and the cash flow statement illustrates how the money earned revenue and whit is did with the money it earned.

To provide information that is specifically targeted and focused, each of the three financial statements must include certain types of information, while excluding certain other types of information. The following chapters provide greater detail, but we will provide a brief overview here.

The Basic Accounting Equation

To begin, all of accounting uses what is known as the "basic accounting equation." The basic accounting equation is:

$$\text{Assets} = \text{Liabilities} + \text{Owner's Equity}$$

As in any mathematical equation, the amounts on either side of the "equal sign" must be the same. For example, using simple math, all of the following equations are correct:

$$1+1+1+1= 4$$
$$2+1+1=4$$

$$7-3=4$$

$$2+2=4$$

However, the following equations are incorrect:

$$1+5=4$$

$$2+2=5$$

The first of the three financial statements is the balance sheet, which shows a calculation of a company's net worth by showing the total value of its assets, the total value of its liabilities, and the total value of its owner's equity. Before the balance sheet can be distributed as an official statement of the company's net worth, the accountant must ensure that the data on the balance sheet conforms to the basic accounting equation, i.e., the total amount of the company's assets must be equal to the sum of its liabilities and owner's equity.

The income statement and the cash flow statement follow from the data included in the balance sheet. Thus, by ensuring first that the balance sheet conforms to the basic accounting equation, the accountant can be assured that the other two financial statements also contain accurate and reliable information.

Trial Balance

As stated earlier, there are six steps in the accounting cycle. The third step of this cycle is the preparation of what is known as a trial balance. The previous section illustrates how the basic accounting equation can help an accountant ensure that the information in a balance sheet is accurate and reliable. Of course, preparing financial statements — including the balance sheet — are the last step of the accounting cycle, so it stands to reason that the accounting cycle includes a mechanism for allowing the accountant to ensure that all the information recorded earlier by the bookkeeper is accurate and reliable. This procedure occurs in Step 3, when the accountant prepares trial balance.

The trial balance is an accounting worksheet that allows the accountant to verify the reliability of the data recorded by the bookkeeper. Although the trial balance is never released to shareholders with the three primary financial statements, it is an integral and indispensable component of the accounting cycle. The trial balance lists all of the accounts included in the general ledger (the accounts that are also listed in the chart of accounts). On the trial balance worksheet, the total closing balances of all the accounts are listed. In addition, these balances are listed as either debit balances or credit balances. So, for example, the closing balance of the cash account may have a debit balance of $2,500, while the closing balance of the accounts payable account may have a credit balance of $2,000. Once the accountant has assembled all of the credit and debt balances for all the company's accounts at the closing of the financial period, he totals all the debits balances at the bottom the debt column and all the credit balances at the bottom of the credit column. As the equations required a company's assets to equal the sum of their liabilities and the owner's equities, a trial balance should result an equal figure for both debits and credits. If the total debit balances are not equal to the total credit balances, then the accountant must either locate errors in the bookkeeping records or enter adjusting entries to bring the books into balance before closing and producing financial statements.

Thus, throughout the professional system of bookkeeping and accounting, there are methods of checking for accuracy and reliability. Ultimately, when the accountant completes the entire accounting cycle, the resulting financial statements will provide the business owner with an accurate and concise picture of all the company's underlying financial activity for any given fiscal period.

Chapter 2: The Balance Sheet

XYZ Company
Balance Sheet
As at 30 June 2010

Current Assets		
Cash at bank	30,000	
Inventory	250,000	
Debtors	75,000	
Total current assets		355,000
Non - Current Assets		
Buildings	550,000	
Plant & equipment	250,000	
Vehicles	120,000	
Total non-current assets		920,000
Total Assets		**1,275,000**
Current Liabilities		
Credit cards	15,000	
Creditors	110,000	
Tax Payable	25,000	
Total current liabilities		150,000
Non-current Liabilities		
Long term loans		700,000
Total Liabilities		**850,000**
Owners Equity		
Capital	100,000	
Retained earnings	250,000	
Current earnings	75,000	
Total Owners Equity		**425,000**

The balance sheet is one of the three main financial statements. (The other two are the income statement and the cash flow statement, both of which will be discussed in the next two chapters. In addition, some companies choose to also include a statement of stockholders' equity. You can read a definition of this fourth type of financial statements in the Glossary in Chapter 15). The balance sheet may also be referred to as a statement of financial position.

Generally, the purpose of a balance sheet is to present an overview of the issuing company's financial position by listing all of the company's assets, liabilities, and equity. The balance sheet possesses a characteristic that is fundamentally different form the income statement and the cash flow statement. Specifically, the balance sheet present financial information about a company that is relevant for a particular point in time only, whereas the income statement and the cash flow statement provide an overview of financial activity that covers a longer period of time — usually an entire year. Thus, because the balance sheet's strength illustrates the liquidity of a company — how much money and other assets they currently possess as opposed to how much money they owe — the balance sheet is often used when considering whether to issue a loan to a business. Of course, many other parties — including current and potential investors, management, suppliers, customers, competitors, and financial regulators — may also request a balance sheet to evaluate a company's current financial position. This chapter explores the three main components of the balance sheet, the many methods of financial analysis used to interpret balance sheet data, and how those analyses may be used by interested parties.

Assets

Remember that the basic accounting equation is **Assets = Liabilities + Owner's Equity**. This section discusses in detail what assets are and how the balance sheet allows accountants to provide information about a company's assets.

In simplest terms, assets all of the property owned by a company that provides some type of value to the company, as expressed in dollars. There are many types and forms of assets. The most obvious example of an asset is cash. If your business uses a checking account to pay bills or for the deposit of money earned from the sale of goods and services, then the balance in the checking account is one of your primary assets. Your company may also have other types of cash accounts, such as a petty cash fund for per diem purchases. So-called "cash equivalent" accounts include short-term investments, such as certificates of deposit. Other financial assets include marketable securities, which are investments in stocks that can be sold for cash within one year.

Assets also include physical property, such as machinery and office furniture. Also referred to as fixed assets, these types of assets include all the major physical property, including office equipment, furniture, and machinery that your business needs to produce its core services. Fixed assets may include:

- Office furniture

- Office equipment
- Supplies
- Inventory
- Machinery
- Tools
- Land
- Land improvements
- Buildings

In addition to cash accounts and fixed assets, your balance sheet will also reflect the value of non-cash financial assets, such as prepaid expenses. These types of financial assets may include:

- Accounts receivable
- Prepaid rent or lease payments
- Prepaid insurance policies
- Prepaid legal fees or retainers
- Prepaid advertising
- Long-term investments (Securities such as stocks that will not be sold for cash.)

Finally, all of the assets listed above are generally classified as tangible assets—they are finite, physically identifiable assets. But assets may also include what are known as "intangible assets." Chapter 9 discuses intangible assets in detail, but we will mention them briefly here. Intangible assets are assets that are not physical—for example a patent, a copyright, an IP address, or a trademark. These assets can also add value to a company's net worth.

Generally, all asset accounts will have a debit balance. This may go against your natural way of thinking about debits. For example, if you use your debit card to make a purchase from your checking account, your balance declines and if you return the item to the store for a refund, your checking account will be credited for the amount of the purchase. However, the terms "debit" and "credit" are used differently in accounting, and depending on the type of account, a debit or a credit balance may indicate either a positive or negative balance.

(Contra accounts are used in accounting to provide accountants with a way to offset potential gains or losses that fall outside the normal course of business. So, contra assets are asset accounts with credit balances that allow accountants to record discrepancies resulting from unpaid accounts receivable, deprecation, etc.)

Accountants follow a specific formula for showing a company's assets on the balance sheet. On a vertical balance sheet, assets are always listed at the top of the balance sheet. On a horizontal balance sheet, they are always listed on the left of the balance sheet. Regardless of whether the balance sheet uses a vertical or horizontal format, assets are listed in the following order:

- Current Assets
  - Cash and cash equivalents
  - Marketable securities
  - Accounts receivable
  - Inventory
  - Prepaid expenses
- Investments
- Fixed Assets (Property, Plant, and Equipment)
- Intangible Assets
- Other Assets

Liabilities

Whereas assets show all the property owned by a company, liabilities shows all of a company's outstanding financial obligations to creditors. Because liability accounts show amounts that must be paid, these accounts often have the word "payable" in the account title. Remember that a balance sheet is controlled by the basic accounting equation: Assets = Liabilities + Owner's Equity. Because we know that the assets are all the property that a company owns, we can think of liabilities as the unpaid portion for the cost of purchasing those assets. Put differently, liabilities are the source of a company's assets.

In addition to money owed, liabilities also include the "Unearned revenues" account. This account includes goods or services for which money has been received, but which have not yet been delivered. Because the company still retains the inventory and has not spent the manpower and resources to provide the goods or services that were sold, this type of income cannot yet be considered an asset, so it is placed in the Unearned Revenue account under Liabilities on the Balance Sheet.

Following are examples of the types of accounts that may be included under liabilities on a balance sheet:

- Accounts Payable

- Notes Payable
- Salaries Payable
- Interest Payable
- Other Accrued Expenses Payable
- Income Taxes Payable
- Customer Deposits
- Warranty Liability
- Lawsuits Payable
- Unearned Revenues
- Bonds Payable

These accounts will be further categorized according to whether they are current liabilities or long-term liabilities. Current liabilities are those liabilities that must be paid within one year from the date of the balance sheet; long-term liabilities are payable at a time beyond one year from the date of the balance sheet.

Liability accounts normally carry a credit balance. And as with asset accounts, contra liability accounts allow accountants to adjust for potential discrepancies resulting from uncertainties in the business environment. (For example, a lender may change the terms of repayment, resulting in a reduction in the amount owed by a company on a note or a bond.) Contra liability accounts normally carry a debit balance and may include accounts such as:

- Discounts on Notes or Bonds Payable
- Debt or Bond Issue Costs

As when reporting assets, accountant must also use standardized formats to report liabilities. On a vertical balance sheet, liabilities will appear under assets; on a horizontal balance sheet, liabilities will appear at the top of the left column. Regardless of whether the accountant uses a vertical or horizontal balance sheet, liabilities will be grouped under the following categories and shown in the following order:

- Current liabilities
  - Accounts payable
  - Accrued expenses
  - Notes payable
  - Wages payable
  - Interest payable
  - Taxes payable
  - Warranty liability
  - Unearned revenues
- Long-term liabilities
  - Notes payable
  - Bonds payable
  - Other long-term debt

Owner's (Stockholders') Equity

As with liabilities, the owner's (or stockholders') equity is also the source of a company's assets. Recalling again the basic accounting equation: Assets=Liabilities + Owner's Equity, the Owner's Equity portion of this equation is often referred to as the "book value" of a company because it reflects the remaining value when the amount that must be paid is subtracted from the value of what is already owned. The residual is the owner's equity in the company — the amount the company would be left with if all liquid assets were sold and converted to cash and all outstanding bills were paid. We can rewrite the basic accounting equation by solving for Owner's Equity to show this relationship:

Assets=Liabilities + Owner's Equity

(Assets) - **Liabilities**=(Liabilities + Owner's Equity) - **Liabilities**

Asset-Liabilities=Owner's Equity

On a balance sheet, the term "Owner's Equity" is used if the business is a sole proprietorship. However, if the company is a corporation — whether publicly traded or privately held — the term Stockholders' Equity is used to reflect the fact that the company is funded in part through the issuance of stocks; thus, there is more than one owner.

The types of accounts in this section of the balance sheet will be different depending on whether the company is a sole proprietorship or a corporation. In a sole proprietorship, owner's equity accounts may include:

- Capital
- Current Year's Net Income

Although the Stockholders' Equity section occupies the same position on the balance sheet and serves the same accounting purpose, the account types will be different than for a sole proprietorship. Types of corporate Stockholders' Equity accounts may include:

- Preferred Stock
- Common Stock
- Paid-in Capital in excess of par value
- Paid-in capital from treasury stock
- Retained Earnings
- Accumulated Other Comprehensive Income

Equity accounts normally have a credit balance, and like both asset and liability accounts, they may be offset by contra accounts to allow the accountant to make adjustments for uncertainties or discrepancies. Contra equity accounts normally carry a debit balance.

Owner's Equity accounts are usually limited in number, but an example of an Owner's Equity contra account may be:

- Drawing (the account from which the owner draws a salary)

Examples of contra accounts for Stockholders' Equity may include:

- Treasury Stock

On both vertical and horizontal balance sheets, the Owner's (Stockholders' Equity) appears just below the Liabilities section; on a horizontal balance sheet, this section will appear on the left side. Although there is no legally-mandated format to which all balance sheets must conform, accounting conventions require that this section of the balance sheet shows Equity accounts in a standardized format, with accounts in order and organized by category.

Generally, Owner's Equity accounts will be organized as follows:

- Capital
- Drawing
- Current Year's Net Income

For Stockholders' Equity, accounts will be organized by category, as follows:

- Paid-in Capital
- Retained Earnings
- Accumulated Other Comprehensive Income

- Treasury Stock

Understanding the Balance Sheet

The balance sheet is unique among the three main financial statements because it represents an aspect of a company's financial condition only for a specific point in time – the date the balance sheet was created. Both the Income Statement and the Cash Flow Statements (discussed in the next 2 chapters) show aspects of a company's financial condition over a period of time. Thus, this "snapshot" of a company's finances that a balance sheet provides is used differently by various financial analysts to gain an understanding of a company's underlying financial structure. Specifically, a balance sheet by itself cannot indicate whether the business is experiencing any trends that develop over a period of time, such as growth in certain areas or losses in certain underperforming sectors. As a result, these types of analyses using a balance sheet can only be made by comparing any given balance sheet with a balance sheet for the same company from a different time period, or with the balance sheets of other businesses in the same industry.

As stated earlier, the primary use of the balance sheet is to indicate the relationship among the three elements of the basic accounting equation. The balance sheet not only allows financial analysts to determine the value of assets owned by a company and the amount of money owed by a company, but also the company's net worth, or "book value."

Accountants can also use balance sheets to create various ratios that communicate information about a company's financial health to potential investors. One such ratio is the debt-to-equity ratio (D/E). The D/E is calculated by dividing the total liabilities by owner's (shareholders') equity. The D/E helps potential investors assess a company's ability to use financial leverage by showing how much of a company's operations are financed by debt as compared to cash or other wholly owned funds. The D/E also shows whether a company would be able to pay off all its debts in the event of total liquidation.

The Net Working Capital Ratio (NWC) represents the difference between a company's current assets and its current liabilities. This ratio measures several aspects of a company's liquidity, such as the efficiency of its operations and its ability to pay bills in the short-term. A company with a positive working capital ratio is more likely to attract investors; a company with a negative NWC may have more difficulty paying its creditors.

Another ratio derived from balance sheets is the acid-test ratio, which helps financial analysts determine whether a company's short-term assets are sufficient to pay for its short-term liabilities. Also called the quick ratio, the acid-test ratio is calculated using the following formula:

$$\text{Acid Test} = \frac{(\text{Cash} + \text{Marketable Securities} + \text{Accounts Receivable})}{\text{Current Liabilities}}$$

The resulting figure derived from dividing these specific assets by current liabilities produces a number greater than or less than 1. If a company's acid test is less than 1, it does not have enough liquid assets to pay its current liabilities. An acid test number that is significantly lower than the NWC indicates that the company's assets are comprised mostly of inventory. While this is generally not a good sign, some retail businesses whose revenue is derived mostly from selling inventory items may have a low acid test number that does not necessarily indicate financial instability.

Chapter 3: The Income Statement

Figure 16: Free Image

Like the balance sheet discussed in Chapter 2, the income statement is one of the three main financial statements. (The other is the cash flow statement, which will be discussed in the next chapter. In addition, some companies choose to also include a statement of stockholders' equity. You can read a definition of this fourth type of financial statements in the Glossary in Chapter 15). The income statement is also known as the statement of operations, the profit and loss statement, the statement of earnings, and the statement of revenue and expense. In many cases, a company may be required to submit an income statement to the Securities and Exchange Commission (SEC) or other financial regulators or financial institutes. In other cases, a company may simply produce an income statement for its own internal uses; these types of income statements are generally referred to as profit and loss statements.

Unlike the balance sheet, which provides a so-called "snapshot" of finances at the time the report is generated, income statements provide information about a company's financial performance over a specified period of time. Specifically, the income statement provides insight into the company's profitability by providing details about its revenues, its expenses, and its resulting profit (or loss). This chapter provides detailed information about the standard format of an income statement, some clarifications about how each section should highlight the company's performance, and some definitions about some of the key terms recorded in the income statement.

Basics of the Income Statement

Income statements are used to assess the profitability of a company over a specified period of time. The time period — which may be a week, three weeks, a month, five months, a year, or any other time interval — is always specified at the top of the income statement. To show a company's profitability, the income statement shows a company's revenues (the amount earned from all activity) and a company's expenses (the amount of money they had to spend to provide goods and services). Generally, the difference between revenues and expenses shows the company's net profit for the time period indicated at the top of the income statement. Although the basic concept of the income statement is easy to understand, a properly formatted income statement is more complicated and involves the use of many accounting principles.

Accrual vs Cash Accounting

First, all income statements must use the accrual method of accounting. The reason for this rule is that the purpose of the income statement is to provide insight into a company's profitability over time, not just the amount of cash it has received or spent at any specific point in time.

We'll use an example to illustrate the difference between cash accounting and accrual accounting. Let's say Smith Tech Repair offers computer maintenance services to all offices operating in the downtown area. In February, Mr. Smith, the owner of Smith Tech Repair, provided routine maintenance for desktop and laptop machines at 1,000 locations; each service session was invoiced at $29.95 for a total of $29,950. The invoices had a due date of March 10. Let's assume further that all of the office managers who received an invoice from Smith Tech Repair paid those invoices on March 10. Using cash accounting, Mr. Smith would record $0.00 in revenue for the month of February, even though he completed 1,000 service contracts; for March, he would record the paid invoices as $29,950 in income, even though the invoices were issued for work completed in February. Thus, cash accounting records income (and expenses) when is paid, not when it is earned (or incurred).

Using the same example, the accrual method of accounting would allow Mr. Smith to record $29,950 as income for the month of February, even though he will not receive the actual funds until March because the funds he received in March reflect income he earned from contracts that were completed in February. This aspect of accounting is known as the revenue recognition principle, which is discussed in greater detail in Chapters 5 and 12.

And as with income, so as with expenses. Let's say Smith had to hire an employee for the month of February to help him complete his service contracts. The employee worked for a total of 20 hours during the month of February, as a rate of $20 per hour. The employee earned $400 in February, and Smith Tech Repair issued a paycheck on March 10. This expense is recorded as a wages payable expense for the Month of February, even though the money does not leave Smith Tech Repair's bank account until March.

Accrual accounting also allows companies to distribute some types expenses over time. Let's assume that Mr. Smith pays $450 per month to rent his office and workspace. He pays the entire cost of annual rent at the beginning of every year, so each January, he writes the building manger a check for $5,400. The check is written and cashed in January, so using the cash accounting method, Mr. Smith would show a January rent expense of $5,400. However, the January rent expense really reflects costs that cover the entire year. By using the accrual method, Mr. Smith can show a rent expense of $450 per month, even though all of the money was paid in January. Thus, in both of these examples, the accrual method allows a company to record its expenses when they are incurred, rather than when they are paid. This principle is known as the matching principle, which is discussed in greater detail in Chapters 5 and 12.

By using the accrual method, the income statement provides a more accurate description of a company's profitability. Investors and financial regulators who examine income statements are less interested in the amount of cash a company received or spent during a given time. Instead, they want to know whether the company's core services are producing revenue, and if so, whether the revenue the company produces is greater than or less than the amount of expenses they must pay to stay in business. Because all businesses provide their services and incur expenses over time, only an accounting method that records transactions over time can provide an accurate assessment of profitability.

Components of an Income Statement

Aside from the accounting method used to create an income statement, an accountant must also know what kind of financial data should be provided on an income statement. As stated earlier, the income statement reports two major categories of financial data — revenues and expenses. However, revenues that are not the same as the total of all cash receipts and expenses may involve more than simply the total of all checks written to pay bills.

There are two methods of creating an income statement — the single-step method and the multiple-step method. We'll examine the single-step method first. Using the single-step method, and income statement reports four main categories of financial data:

- Revenues
- Expenses
- Gains
- Losses

At the bottom of the Income Statement is the so-called "bottom line," which shows the company's Net Income for the period indicated at the top of the Income statement. We'll begin this section with a brief overview of what each of these categories of financial data includes before examining specific differences in terminology in greater detail.

Revenue

First, the Revenue section shows all amounts earned by a company from both operating and non-operating activities:

- Operating revenue is all revenue in a reporting period earned from a company's main activities. For example, for a manufacturer, wholesaler, or retailer, their operating revenue will reflect the amount of money they earned during the reporting period from product sales. Alternatively, a business that provides services — such as computer or automotive repair or legal services — operating revenue will reflect the amount of money during the reporting period earned as a direct result of providing those services.

- Non-operating revenue is money that business earns as a result of activity that is secondary to its core activities. Whether a company sells goods or services or both, the non-operating revenue section reports all money earned as a result of activity that is secondary to selling goods and services. For example, is a business has placed money in an interest-bearing account, the interest earned would be recorded as non-operating revenue. Similarly, if a business owns rental properties, the rental payments would be reported as non-operating revenue. Other types of non-operating revenue include royalty payments for copyrights or income from advertising sources.

Expenses

Next, the Expenses section of an income statement includes both primary and secondary expenses:

- Primary expenses are all expenses incurred as a result of generating operating revenue. Primary expenses are generally grouped into the following four main categories:
  - Cost of Goods Sold (CoGS)
  - Selling, general, and administrative expenses (SG&A)
  - Depreciation and Amortization
  - Research and development (R&D)
  - The specific expenses themselves may cover a die range of primary operating business activity, such as:
  - Employee wages
  - Sales commissions
  - Utility payments for telephone, electricity, etc.
  - Transportation and maintenance
- Secondary expenses are all expenses incurred as a result of business activity that is not directly related to the business's main, core goods

and services. Secondary expenses may include costs such as:

- ○   Interest payments on loans
- ○   Bank fees.

Gains and Losses

Finally the income statement also records Gains and Losses. Gains are a form of income and losses are a form of expense, but the income statements separate them out to show specifically how a company is either earning money or spending money. Gains and losses generally occur as a result of a one-time sale of some type of asset for an amount of money that is different from its "book value."

- Gains result from the sale of an asset such as a company van, a company-owned building like a warehouse, in which the company is able to sell the item for more than its current market value. Gains may also result from the sale of investment securities that result in a net profit over the purchase price.
- Losses also result for the sale of assets. For example, if a company is forced to sell a vehicle that was damaged, or lost money in the sale of

an investment security, the result would be recorded as a loss on the income statement.

Thus, gains can be considered a form of revenue, and losses can be considered a form of expense. However, gains and losses different from both operating and non-operating revenue, as well as from primary and secondary expenses because they result from special, one-time transactions, rather than routine business activity. By providing a separate place for these data on the income statement, investors, managers, and financial regulators can more accurately assess a company's strengths and weaknesses in terms of its profitability.

Net Income

Finally, when all of the revenue, expenses, gains, and losses that a company has incurred are accurately recorded in the appropriate section of the income statement, the bottom line shows the total net income for that company for the period of time specified at the top of the statement. The formula for calculating a company's net income is:

Net Income = (Revenue + Gains) – (Expenses + Losses)

Format of an Income Statement

As with all financial statements, the financial data on an income statement must be presented according to the established conventions of the accounting profession. Generally a single-step income statement should report financial data in the following order:

-                 Revenues and Gains
-                 Expenses and Losses
-                 Net Income

Following is a very simple example of how a single-step income statement may be calculated:

ABC Goods and Services
Income Statement
For the Six Months Ending June 30, 2019

Revenues and Gains

Sales Revenue	$150,000.00
Intrest earned	$3,000.00
Sale of assets	$2,500.00
Total Revenue and Gains	$155,500.00

Expenses and Losses

Cost of Goods Sold	$100,000.00
Wages and Commissions	$10,000.00
Office supplies	$1,000.00
Utilities and rent	$2,500.00
Interest paid	$750.00
Loss from asset sale	$1,000.00
Total expenses and losses	$115,250.00

Net income $40,250.00

Of course, not all income statement's use the single-step method. The multiple-step income statement allows for a more complex expression of the relationships among a company's revenue sources, expenses, gains, and losses by multiple calculations that involve several subtraction operations to arrive at the net income. The multiple-step income statement calculates separate totals for operating revenues and operating expenses, and for non-operating revenues, expenses, gains and losses. It also includes a section for gross profit; this figure expresses the difference between sales revenue and the cost of goods sold.

The multiple-step income statement uses three steps to arrive at the net income:

1.   Calculate the gross profit
2.   Calculate the operating income
3.   Calculate the net income

These aspects of the multiple-step income statement are discussed in more detail in the next section. But first, the following simple example illustrates show a multiple-step income statement differs from a single-step income statement:

ABC Goods and Services
Income Statement
For the Six Months Ending June 30, 2019

Operating revenue				
Sales				$150,000.00
Cost of Good Sales Revenue				$100,000.00
Gross profit				$50,000.00
Operating expenses				
Sales expenses				
	Advertising	$2,250.00		
	Commissions and wages	$10,000.00	$12,250.00	
Administrative expesnes				
	Office supplies	$1,000.00		
	Utilities and rent	$2,500.00	$3,500.00	
Total operating expenses			$15,750.00	
Operating income			$34,250.00	
Non-operating income and expenses				
Non-operating interest revenue			$750.00	
Gain from asset sale			$3,000.00	
Intrest expenses			-$500.00	
Loss from asset sale			-$250.00	
Total non-opertaing revenue and expenses			$3,000.00	
Net income			$37,250.00	

Understanding the Income Statement

The income statement provides a useful method for allowing managers, financial regulators, and potential investors with an opportunity to gauge the profitability of a company's operating activities. A single-step income statement provides simple and clear picture of how a company's revenues are earned, and whether they are generating enough revenue to earn a profit after paying expenses. A multiple-step income statement provides a far more explicit view of a company's income and expenses and is usually favored by large corporations, especially those who are required to submit financial statement to the SEC.

Like the balance sheet, the data included on a company's income statement can be used to generate many types of ratios and other calculations useful not only in determining opportunities to increase a company's current profitability, but also to determine a company's future potential for growth. This section examines the significance of information included in an income statement and how it can help managers and investors understand a company's operations.

Gross Profit and Cost of Goods Sold

Especially if your company is a retailer that buys goods wholesale then sells them for a profit, the Cost of Goods Sold, or CoGS, is the amount of money the company pays the wholesaler to purchase inventory. Of course, not all companies earn revenue by purchasing inventory wholesale then selling it for a profit at retail prices. Regardless, no matter what kind of business model you are operating, you should be able to indicate a CoGS on your income statement. For example, if your company manufactures and sells items of apparel, the raw materials, machinery, and wages you must pay for to produce finished items of clothing would be considered the CoGS. Service companies may also be able to claim billable hours and employee training as among their CoGS expenses.

Thus, it is inaccurate to assume we can determine a company's profits simply by looking for the total revenue earned. This figure may be important, but the income statement shows a refined understanding of income and expense figures. Look at the example of the multiple-step income statement above. It shows a figure for Gross Profit under operating revenue. The gross profit is an unrefined estimate of a company's earnings over a period of time. The gross profit results from subtracting the CoGS from the total sales revenue.

Aside from serving as the initial calculation toward figuring the net income for the reporting period, the gross profit figures also serve another valuable purpose — they allow investors, managers, and regulators to monitor a company's gross margin. Sometimes used interchangeably with gross profit, the gross margin is actually gross profit expressed as a percentage. In the example above, the gross margin is 33% ($50,000/$150,000). Readers of financial reports may monitor a company's gross margin to determine whether they are sustaining their profitability.

Operating Income Vs. Net Income

As discussed earlier, operating income indicates the amount of income a company earns as a direct result of its core business functions. In the multiple-step income statement above, we can see that the operating income for ABC Goods and Service is $34,250 for the reporting period indicated. Notice that the operating income is different from the operating revenue. Operating income considers income not only net sales, but all financial activity related to core business. Using this example, the operating income is less than gross profit because it accounts for all the administrative and related expenses associated with running the business. Thus, the formula for Operating Income is Gross **Profit – Operating Expenses = Operating Income**.

Of course, larger corporations are usually involved in a wide variety of financial activity. Mergers and acquisitions; securities investments and reinvestment of revenue; asset purchases such as land, buildings, and vehicles; and many other types of financial activity may also generate income for a company. Smaller companies may also earn residual income from rental properties, investments in certificates of deposit, or interest earned on business checking and savings accounts. As a result, the operating income alone does not provide an accurate assessment of a company's total revenue.

The income statement above shows very clearly that ABC Goods and Services was able to generate an additional $3,000 in net revenue from non-operating activities. This information in itself is helpful to anyone seeking a clearer understanding of the company's financial standing by reading the income statement. But perhaps, more importantly, the income statement can be used to calculate a ratio between the net income and the operating income — the larger percentage that a company's net income results from operating income, the less the company is depending on financial activity not related to the core business. In the above example, 92% of the ABC's net income results from operating income; this high percentage can signal to investors that the company is not depending on outside investments to maintain profitability.

Retained Earnings and Dividends

The examples in this section provide a straightforward sample of the standard format and organization of information on an income statement. In the real world, a major global corporation will likely have a tremendous amount of financial activity that needs to be accounted for. A well-designed income statement may make all that accounting appear uncomplicated on the surface, but it is important to remember that financial statements represent the final product, not the potential arduous process of understanding where to place each type of financial transaction record.

The following image shows an income statement form Amazon, Inc:

AMAZON.COM, INC.
CONSOLIDATED STATEMENTS OF OPERATIONS
(in millions, except per share data)

	Year Ended December 31,		
	2015	2016	2017
Net product sales	$ 79,268	$ 94,665	$ 118,573
Net service sales	27,738	41,322	59,293
Total net sales	107,006	135,987	177,866
Operating expenses			
Cost of sales	71,651	88,265	111,934
Fulfillment	13,410	17,619	25,249
Marketing	5,254	7,233	10,069
Technology and content	12,540	16,085	22,620
General and administrative	1,747	2,432	3,674
Other operating expense, net	171	167	214
Total operating expenses	104,773	131,801	173,760
Operating income	2,233	4,186	4,106
Interest income	50	100	202
Interest expense	(459)	(484)	(848)
Other income (expense), net	(256)	90	346
Total non-operating income (expense)	(665)	(294)	(300)
Income before income taxes	1,568	3,892	3,806
Provision for income taxes	(950)	(1,425)	(769)
Equity-method investment activity, net of tax	(22)	(96)	(4)
Net income	$ 596	$ 2,371	$ 3,033
Basic earnings per share	$ 1.28	$ 5.01	$ 6.32
Diluted earnings per share	$ 1.25	$ 4.90	$ 6.15
Weighted-average shares used in computation of earnings per share:			
Basic	467	474	480
Diluted	477	484	493

Using this example, we will consider two examples of how creating an income statement may require that you reconsider how you categorize certain forms of income and expense.

Retained Earnings Are Not the Same as Cash

First, it may be tempting to think of a company's Retained Earnings as simply another component of its revenues. If your company shows retained earnings on your balance sheet under Shareholders' Equity, you may look for a place to include this figure as part of your operating income—after all, logic dictates that all money earned as a result of core business activities should be included in operating revenue. However, while retained earnings result from revenue, they are not the same as cash. Retained earnings earned from revenue are those finds specifically designated for future use, usually to pay dividends to shareholders. As a result, a company's retained earnings are more closely related to their net income because it represents the net income a company saves over time.

In the above example, Amazon's net income for 2015 was $596 million; their retained earnings would be determined as a percentage of that net income that was held for future use.

Dividends Are Not an Expense

One of the most common uses of Retained Earnings is to pay dividends to shareholders. Whereas the first two examples in this section provided a clear illustration of how a company's net income is the difference between its gross profit and its operating expenses, plus any additional non-operating revenue (or losses). However, neither of these simpler examples discussed how income taxes and dividend payments also affect a company's bottom line.

Using the more realistic example of Amazon's income statement, notice that the figure for net income appears below the figure for "Income before income taxes." Thus, after all operating and non-operating expenses are accounted for, the Income Statement must also show how the actual net income will be affected by taxes. So, the net income is the result of subtracting the amount of income tax due from pre-tax income. But before this final amount can be carried forward to the Retained Earnings account, the amount for dividends due to shareholders must be deducted. Thus, dividends are not an expense of business operations, so much as a deduction from Retained Earnings.

Chapter 4: The Cash Flow

Statement

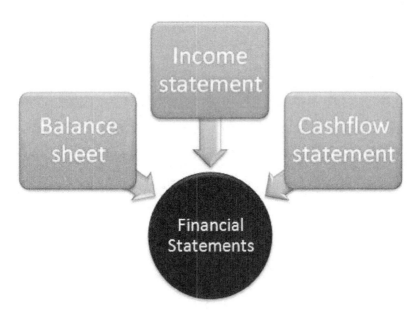

Figure 17: Free Image

The cash flow statement is the third of the three main financial statements. (The other two are the balance sheet and the income statement, both of which are discussed in the preceding two chapters. In addition, some companies choose to also include a statement of stockholders' equity. You can read a definition of this fourth type of financial statements in the Glossary in Chapter 15). The cash flow statement is also known as the statement of cash flows or funds flow statement.

Like the income statement, the cash flow statement shows a company's financial condition over a specified period of time. The essential difference between the income statement and the cash flow statement is that the income statement shows whether a company is profitable; the cash flow statement shows whether a company is liquid. In other words, an income statement may tell you whether or not a company earned money or lost money during a given period of time, but a chase flow statement will show exactly how money was earned or spent. Cash flow statements separates the activities of a company into three main sections—operating activities, investing activities, and financing activities. In addition, there are two methods of generating a cash flow statement—the direct method, which is generally used with cash-based accounting systems and the indirect method, which utilizes accrual-based accounting and incorporates information from the balance statement and the income statement. This chapter discusses the specific features of a cash flow statement and how the information in cash flow statement may be used to evaluate a company's performance.

What is a Cash Flow Statement?

The cash flow statement is also known as the statement of cash flows or statement of funds flows. The cash flow statement bridges the gaps between the income statement and the balance sheet.

Remember that the income statement is created using the accrual method of accounting; thus, it reports not only revenue that has been received, but also revenue that has been earned and invoiced. Similarly, the income records all expenses—both those that have been billed and those that have been paid. Remember also that the balance sheet include both accounts receivable and accounts payable in its calculation of a company's total book value. In addition, the balance sheet indicates the company's value at one specific point in time.

Investors or financial regulators who wanted to make a determination about how much of a company's revenue had already been received and how much of that revenue resulted from cash transactions earned through operating activities, the core services of the business, could use the information included in the balance sheet and the income statement and then make adjustments to the figures to account for credit purchases, investment income, tax liabilities, etc. However, because the cash flow statement is designed with this goal in mind, many investors and creditors will simply request a cash flow statement to understand how the company manages its financial resources, where its money is coming from, how those funds are being spent, and whether the company has enough cash on hand to pay its current outstanding debt obligations. These determinations are difficult enough to assess by simply reviewing financial data. For this reason, the cash flow statement is always required as one of the three major types of financial statements.

The cash flow statement is separated into three main components:

- Cash earned from operating activities
- Cash earned from investing activities
- Cash earned from financing activities

In addition, a fourth component is sometimes included, particularly when cash flow statements are prepared according to the GAAP:

- Disclosure of noncash activities

These sections of the cash flow statement illustrates the important distinction between this type of report and the income statement and balance sheet. Specifically, the cash flow statement deliberately excludes the amount of future incoming and outgoing cash from transactions that have been recorded as credit. Thus, although net income provides an accurate assessment of how much money a company has made after all expenses are accounted for, net income is not the same as cash because it includes both cash and credit sales and expenses.

Cash flow statements may be used for a variety of reasons. For example, by comparing cash from operating activities to cash from net income, an investor can assess the quality of a company's earnings. Specifically, if cash income from operating activities is consistently higher than net income, then the company's earnings may be described as "high quality"; whereas, a company whose operating activities produce less than their net income may cause serious concern among investors. Second, for investors who believe that "cash is king," a cash flow statement can help investors see whether a company is generating more cash than it is using. Such companies will have greater resources to reinvest in the company, making them a more attractive prospect.

Adjusting Data for the Cash Flow Statement

The three sections at the end of this chapter discuss each of the components of the cash flow statement in turn. But before examining those aspects, this section discusses how the financial data in the balance sheet and the income statement are adjusted for the cash flow statement. Essentially, accountants will adjust balance sheet and income statement items to revenue, expenses, and credit using addition or subtraction. These adjustments allow accountants to reevaluate whether the totals on these two types of financial reports results for cash or non-cash transactions and whether they should appear on the cash flow statement.

The following sections discuss how some types of accounts are adjusted prior to their inclusion on the cash flow statement:

Accounts receivable

Accountants must evaluate the balances of accounts receivable sections of balance sheet for more than one period to make adjustments for the cash flow statement. For example, if the accounts receivable balance on a company's balance sheet for January is higher than the accounts receivable balance for the same company's balance sheet in June, this change indicates that more cash has entered the company as a result of customers paying their credit balances. In this case, the accountant will add the amount of the decrease to the total for net sales. On the other hand, if the accounts receivable balance for the same period increases, the amount of the increase is deducted from net sales to show the decrease in cash revenue.

Inventory

Assessing changes in inventory for inclusion on the cash flow statement are slightly more complex. An increase in inventory value on a company's balance sheet from one reporting period to the next indicates that company has spent money to purchase raw materials or wholesale goods. That increased value must be deducted from net sales, but only is the inventory was purchased with cash. Conversely, if the value of inventory decreases, the value of the decrease is added to net sales. However, if inventory was purchased with credit, the balance sheet will show an increase in accounts payable with a corresponding increase in the value of the inventory from one reporting period the next added to net sales.

Accounts payable

Whether the account is taxes payable, wages, payable, or prepaid expenses such as insurance, balances of accounts payable accounts that have been paid off from one reporting period to the next must be subtracted from net income. If accounts payable have not yet been paid off, any differences is in closing balances from one reporting period to the next must be added to net earnings.

Adjustment methods

Adjustments are made using one of two methods:

- Direct cash flow method
- Indirect cash flow method

Direct Cash Flow Method

The direct cash flow method uses actual cash flow data taken directly from a given company's operations and present cash flow data according to gross classifications of cash receipts and payments. For example, using the direct method, the accountant will gather all transaction records and cash receipts showing cash payments made to suppliers, cash receipts shoeing sales to customers, and records of salary payments to employees. Totals for inclusion on the cash flow statement result from calculating beginning and ending balances of the applicable accounts, then assessing the net increase or decrease in their value over the course of the applicable accounting period.

Indirect Cash Flow Method

The indirect method derives financial data from the balance sheet and the income statement and comparing changes in the various account types from one reporting period to the next. Both the balance sheet and the income statement are calculated using the accrual method, so certain adjustments have to be made to the totals to ensure they reflect only cash transactions. For example, because the net income figure on the income statement includes income that may have been earned but not yet received. As a result, the accountant must adjust for earnings before interest and taxes (EBIT) so he or she can isolate cash income and deduct amounts from accounts receivable. In addition, non-operating activities like depreciation that do not affect cash flow must also be included when using the indirect cash flow method.

Components of the Cash Flow Statement

Cash Flow from Operating Activities

The first section of the cash flow statement reports cash from operating activities. This section shows all cash payment received and all cash payments made by a company in support of its operating activities, which are all those business activities directly related to the daily maintenance of its core business functions. For example, for a hardware store, operating activities would include all sales of merchandise from the store's inventory, payment of employee wages, rent and utility payments for the store facility, and all tax and interest payments related to these activities. Other types of financial activity not directly related to operating activities are included in the other two sections of the cash flow statement—investing activities and financing activities. The following types of financial records result from operating activities:

- Cash receipts from sales of goods and services
- Interest payments
- Income tax payments
- Payments made to suppliers for inventory or raw materials used for production
- Salary and wage payments to employees
- Rent and utility payments
- Transportation costs directly related to operating activities
- Accounts Receivable

- Inventory
- Supplies
- Prepaid Insurance
- Accounts Payable
- Unearned Revenues
- Other Current Liabilities

Investment companies, whose goods and services are comprised entirely of securities and other financial products and services, may also include cash receipts for sales of loans or other debt and equity instruments.

Because operating activities represent the main source of a business's revenue generation, this section is generally considered to be the most important section of the cash flow statement. Positive cash flow over time indicates a company in healthy financial condition. The stronger the positive cash flow, the healthier the financial condition of the company. Financial data on the operating activities of a cash flow statement are reported in the following order:

- Net earnings (The net income figure taken directly from the income statement.)
- Additions to cash:
  - Depreciations
  - Decrease in accounts receivable

- Increase in accounts payable
- Increase in taxes payable
- Etc.
- Subtractions from cash:
  - Increase in inventory
  - Increase in accounts receivable
  - Decrease in accounts payable
  - Etc.
- Net cash from operations.

Cash Flow from Investing Activities

This section of the cash flow statement records changes in the value of equipment, fixed assets, or other financial instruments. Changes in cash flow resulting from investing activity records how much money has been spent or generated as a result of making investments during specified period of time.

Depending on the type, size, and complexity of your business, you may include some or all of these types of investment activities. There are many other types of investment activities not listed here that may also appear on your cash flow statement.

In addition, the following types of financial activity should NOT appear in the investing activities section of the cash flow statement:

- Interest payments
- Dividend payments
- Financing data related to debt or equity
- Depreciation of fixed assets
- Any income or expenses that are part of operating activities

Generally, transactions in this section of the cash flow statement are reported in the following order:

- Purchases of property, plant, and equipment (PP&E)
- Income from the sale of PP&E
- Purchases for the acquisition of other companies or businesses
- Income from the sale of other companies or businesses
- Purchases of investment securities, such as stocks and bonds
- Income from the sale of investment securities

Cash Flow from Financing Activities

Finally, this section of the cash flow statement records changes in long-term liability and stockholders' equity, such as debt, loans, stock options, and other forms of financing, from one reporting period to the next. Any company that needs to raise money must do so using equity (by issuing shares) or debt (by taking out loans). Changes to both new and existing financing activities will be shown on the cash flow statement.

Whereas the operating activities section shows how much net cash a company has generated over time, and the investing activities section shows how that company has spent the money it has generated, the financing activities section shows how a company funds its overall operations.

The following types of accounts may be included in the financing activities section of the cash flow statement:

- Issuance of equity
- Repayment of equity
- Dividend payments
- Issuance of debt through new loans
- Debt repayment
- Lease payments on capital investments
- Bonds Payable
- Deferred Income Taxes
- Preferred Stock
- Paid-in Capital in Excess of Par-Preferred Stock

- Common Stock
- Paid-in Capital in Excess of Par-Common Stock
- Paid-in Capital from Treasury Stock
- Retained Earnings
- Treasury Stock

In this section of the cash flow statement, activities are recorded as an inflow of cash when capital is raised and as an outflow of cash when dividends are paid. For example, if a company issues bonds for public purchase, the company will revive cash when investors purchase the bonds; however, the company must also pay interest to the bondholders, which results in a cash outflow in this section of the cash flow statement.

Generally, financial data in this section of the cash flow statement is reported in the following order:
- Income received from issuing long-term debt
- Cash outflow for repayment of long-term debt
- Cash outflow for principal repayments of capital lease obligations
- Cash outflow for principal repayments of finance lease obligations

Sample Cash Flow Statement

The following illustration provides a simple example of how cash statement illustrates changes in the cash value of the different areas of a company's business activities over time. The top figure shows an example of a cash flow statement that uses the direct method, and the bottom figure shows a cash flow statement that uses the indirect method. Notice how the primary difference in these two statements is that the figures for operating activities using the direct method are derived directly from the business daily transactions; whereas, the operating activities section using the indirect method requires a refinement of data taken from the balance sheet and income statement.

Direct Method:

Operating Activities

Cash received from customers	$800
Cash paid to suppliers	(150)
Employee compensations	(200)
Other operating expenses paid	(250)
Net cash from operating activities	200

Investing Activities

Sale of land	200
Purchase of equipment	(300)
Net cash from investing activities	(100)

Financing Activities

Common share dividends	(200)
Payment on long-term debt	(300)
Net cash from financing activities	(500)
Beginning Cash Balance	X
Ending Cash Balance	Y

Indirect Method:

Operating Activities

Net Income	$50,000
Add: Depreciation expense	$10,000
Decrease in AR	$2,000
Increase in inventory	$3,000
Decrease in prepaid expense	$4,000
Increase in accounts payable	$5,000
Net Cash provided by operating activities	$XXX

Investing Activities

Sale of land	200
Purchase of equipment	(300)
Net cash from investing activities	(100)

Financing Activities

Common share dividends	(200)
Payment on long-term debt	(300)
Net cash from financing activities	(500)
Beginning Cash Balance	X
Ending Cash Balance	Y

Chapter 5: Generally Accepted Accounting Principles

Figure 18: Free Image

Generally Accepted Accounting Principles — or GAAP — is a term used to describe a set of rules and standards that govern the accounting profession. Consider the vast number of privately and publicly held businesses in operation on any given day. From small, local retail and service businesses, to medium-sized companies that operate in more than one city or state to major multinational corporations, the variations in the types of goods and services offered and the complex demands and needs of investors and other interested parties require some type of standardized financial reporting. If each company simply maintained and produced accounting records and reports according to its own individually developed accounting techniques and philosophies, investors, banks, managers and financial regulators would have to spend more time trying to understand each company's accounting and bookkeeping methods than the information actually contained in their financial statements.

The GAAP govern the practice of accounting in three major areas: basic accounting principles and guidelines, rules and standards determined by the Financial Standards Accounting Board (FASB), and generally accepted industry practices that have evolved over time. The FASB, the Securities and Exchange Commission (SEC), the American Institute of CPAs (AICPA), and the Governmental Accounting Standards Board (GASB) all contribute to the rules and standards of the GAAP. The GASB and the FAF, in turn, are administered by the Financial Accounting Foundation (FAF). The GAAP is used primarily with the United States. Internationally, companies usually conform to the International Financial Reporting Standards (IFRS). This chapter discusses some of the specifics relating to each of these regulatory agencies, the various principles included under the GAAP, and the differences between the GAAP and the IFRS.

What Are Generally Accepted Accounting Principles (GAAP)?

The GAAP are concepts, principles, and conventions that govern the format and content of financial statements. Depending on the size and complexity of the business, the laws of the United States may require a company to release these financial statements on a regular basis and submit them to regulatory agencies such as the SEC. The ten principles of the GAAP are:

- Principle of regularity: To maintain compliance with the GAAP, financial statements accountants and their financial statements must always demonstrate strict adherence to established regulations.

- Principle of consistency: All accounting standards apply to all entities throughout the financial reporting process.

- Principle of sincerity: Accountants must be committed to producing financial statements that are accurate, impartial, and free of bias or conflict of interest.

- Principle of permanence of methods: GAAP-compliant accountants must adhere consistently to the same uniform set of procedures to prepare financial reports and statements.

- Principle of non-compensation: All financial statements, must report complete coverage of off all a business entity's transactions. Positive reports must be produced free of inducements through compensation or reward; negative reports must be produced free of the fear of retaliation or sanction.

- Principle of prudence: GAAP-compliant accountants may not allow speculation to influence their reporting of financial data.

- Principle of continuity: GAAP-compliant financial statements that include asset valuations assume that the organization's operations will continue.

- Principle of periodicity: GAAP-compliant accountants must report revenues according to standard accounting time periods, such as fiscal quarters or fiscal years.

- Principle of materiality: All GAAP-compliant financial reports must fully disclose an organization's financial condition.

- Principle of utmost good faith: All parties involved in the production of GAAP-compliant financial statements will be assumed to be acting with complete honesty.

Who are the SEC, the AICPA, the FASB and the GASB?

All of these organizations are financial regulatory agencies administered either by the federal government or by independent advisory boards. Each of them has a specific concentration, and all of them work together to ensure that all business transactions and financial activity are conducted according to established principles and methods and according to laws. These organizations not only work with governmental law-making, they may also have the authority to enforce laws, investigate complaints of criminal activity, impose sanctions and other penalties against businesses who operate outside the law or fail to comply with established standards. Together, ensure stability and legal compliance in business and financial transactions and dealings. This section provides a brief overview of each of these agencies in turn, including the degree to which they contribute to the formation and enforcement of the GAAP.

Securities and Exchange Commission

The Securities and Exchange Commission — the SEC — is an agency within the federal government of the United States of America. The official mission of the SEC is "to protect investors; maintain fair, orderly, and efficient markets; and facilitate capital formation. The SEC strives to promote a market environment that is worthy of the public's trust" (About the Division of Enforcement, 2007). The SEC has seven major divisions:

- Corporation Finance
- Enforcement
- Investment Management
- Economic and Risk Analysis
- Trading and Markets
- Office of Administrative Law Judges
- Office of Compliance Inspections and Examinations

All of these divisions share responsibility for enforcing laws that affect both domestic and international business transactions, particularly investment transactions. The Division of Corporation Finance, in particular, has issued recent rulings governing the use of GAAP accounting principles in financial statements released to investors. A recent release from April 2018 entitled, "Non-GAAP Financial Measures," provides the SEC's detailed responses to the types of financial statements that may violate certain laws enforced by the SEC if they do not comply with GAAP principles.

The American Institute of Certified Public Accountants (AICPA)

The AICPA was founded in 1897 to represent the interests of the accounting profession. Since its founding, the accounting profession has been an established and recognized force in ensuring this field is regulated by rigorous educational requirements, high professional standards, a strict adherence to ethical conduct and a commitment to serving the public interest.

As a certification body, the AICPA develops and grades performance on the Uniform CPA Examination. As a regulatory agency, the AICPA monitors and enforces compliance with the standards of the accounting profession. Today, the AICPA provides advocacy services for the accounting profession before legislative bodies, public interest groups and other professional associations. In addition, the AICPA is responsible for developing standards and rules for conducting audits of private companies, as well as many of the other responsibilities of professional CPAs. The AICPA also provides educational material and guidance for members.

The Financial Accounting Standards Board (FASB)

The FASB was founded in 1973. The FASB is a non-profit private-sector regulatory agency with headquarters in Norwalk, CT. The FASB's main function is to establish the accounting and reporting standards for all companies — whether public sector or private sector — and all non-profit organizations that adhere to GAAP. Both the SEC and the AICPA have recognized the authority of the FASB. The SEC regards the FASB as the official regulatory body overseeing the accounting standards of public companies.

The FASB operates in cooperation with the Financial Accounting Foundation (FAF) and the Governmental Accounting Standards Board (GASB). The FAF is also an independent, private-sector, non-profit organization and oversees the administration of both the FASB and the GASB. Together with the FAF and the GASB, the FASB's mission is to ensure that financial accounting and reporting standards are upheld and that investors and other stakeholders have access to understand how those standards apply.

The Governmental Accounting Standards Board (GASB)

The GASB was established in 1984. Also based in Norwalk, CT, and also an independent, private-sector, non-profit organization, the GASB establishes accounting and financial reporting standards for American state and local governments agencies that adhere to the GAAP.

The GASB's authority as a regulatory body is recognized by the AICPS, as well as state and local governments and state boards of accountancy. The GASB develops accounting standards in collaboration with the FASB and the FAF. The FAF also oversees the administration, financing, and appointments within the GASB.

Differences Between U.S. Accounting Standards and International Accounting Standards

The GAAP accounting framework is used predominantly by companies and organizations that operate within the United States. Publicly held companies within the United States that are regulated by the SEC may be required to issue GAAP-compliant financial statements. Other companies may choose to conform to GAAP accounting standards as a means of establishing trust among investors and other interested parties. The GAAP have been codified into the Accounting Standards Codification (ASC), the official statement of GAAP policy issued by the FASB.

Although the GAAP is recognized internationally, most countries outside the United States use the International Financial Reporting Standards (IFRS) framework. Whereas the GAAP is heavily dependent on complex and detailed rules, the IFRS focus is on general principles. As a result, IFRS documentation is a much smaller body of legislative work that then the GAAP. Although the IFRS as a result is easier to understand and potentially easier to apply than the GAAP, the GAAP is regarded as for more comprehensive.

Currently, some regulatory agencies are making an effort to bridge gaps between these two accounting frameworks, with an eventual goal of reducing the number and complexity of differences. Although some regulatory bodies believe the two frameworks should eventually be merged, others have voiced dissent leading to the significant possibility that these frameworks will remain separate and independent.

Chapter 6: Double-Entry

Accounting

Figure 19: Free Image

Double-entry accounting uses a system of recording transactions that requires two entries for every transaction — one entry shows where money came from; the other entry shows where money went. These entries are called debits and credits, and for every transaction, the total amount debited muse be the same as the total amount credited. Because two entries are required for every transaction, it is called double-entry accounting. The counterpart of double-entry accounting is single-entry accounting. Most people who manage their personal finances — as when balancing their checkbook when paying their monthly household expenses — use single-entry accounting. With single-entry accounting, only one entry is required for each transaction — if you make a deposit to your savings account, you simply write in the amount of the deposit and update the balance; if you write a check to pay a bill, you simply write the amount of the check and deduct it from the balance in your account. Most people don't consider that there is a second part of these transactions — in the first example, the money you placed in your savings account had to come from somewhere, and in the second example, although you decreased the balance in your checking account, you also decreased the total amount you own in bills for the month. Double-entry accounting requires the accountant to ensure that both sides of every transaction are recorded. The result is a more accurate picture of money management, and financial statements that contain a more detailed analysis of a company's financial condition.

Understanding the general principle of double-entry accounting is easy enough. In actual practice, there are considerable complexities, and you may have to relearn some of the terminology you have grown accustomed to—especially the use of the terms, "debit" and "credit." However, with a little diligence and patience, anyone can learn to use the double-entry system of accounting. In addition, because double-entry accounting is generally required for adherence to GAAP standards, learning to use this system earlier rather than later can help your business succeed. This chapter covers several important aspects of double-entry accounting, including debits and credits, general journal entries, general ledger entries, and the trial balance.

Debits and Credits

Before considering debits and credits themselves, consider
that accounting groups all transactions into separate accounts.
Chapters 1, 2, and 3 discussed the basics of accounting from a
general perspective. Chapter 1 discussed that all of the
accounts used to record a business's daily transactions are
listed in the chart of accounts. Chapter 4 discussed how the
balance sheet shows all of the accounts that comprise a
company's assets, liabilities, and equity. Chapter 3 discussed
how the income statement incorporates in accounts resulting
from revenue, expenses, gains, and losses. Thus, however
many individual accounts may be listed on a chart of
accounts, all those individual accounts will fall into one of
seven categories:

- Assets
- Liabilities
- Equities
- Revenue
- Expenses
- Gains
- Losses

In accounting, a debit does not always decrease the balance of an account, and a credit does not always increase the balance of an account. Instead, debits are transaction entries placed on the left side of an account ledger, and credits are transaction entries placed on the right side of an account ledger. (The next sections discuss journals and ledgers in more detail.) Whether a debit or a credit either decreases or increases the balance of an account depends on which of the seven types of accounts listed above has been either debited or credited. For example, debiting an asset account increases the balance, but debiting either a liability or equity account decreases the balance. However, regardless of the type of account, the total debits and credits for every single transaction must be equal.

The following two charts will help you remember how debits and credits affect the various types of accounts:

Account Type	Increased By	Decreased By
Assets	Debit	Credit
Expenses	Debit	Credit
Liabilities	Credit	Debit
Equity	Credit	Debit
Revenue	Credit	Debit

Debits	Credits
Increase asset and expense accounts	Increase liability, equity, and revenue accounts
Decrease liability, equity, and revenue accounts	Decrease asset and expense accounts
Always recorded on the left side of the ledger	Always recorded on the right side of the account ledger

Examples of double-entry accounting

To use double-entry accounting accurately and effectively, the accountant must be able to determine which accounts are affected by every transaction. Every transaction involves money leaving one account, and money being added to another account. As a result, when an accountant records a transaction, he or she must be able to determine which account the money was taken from and which account money was taken and into which account money was deposited for the transaction to have been completed.

Let's suppose a mobile tech repair business purchase a fleet vans for its service technicians. The company purchased the vans on credit, and spent a total of $300,000. These vans have an estimated useful life of at least 10 years, so they are considered a fixed asset. An accountant using single-entry accounting might simply add the total purchase price to the outstanding balance of the company's line of credit. However, using double-entry accounting, the accountant must determine the cash inflow and the cash outflow, both of which must be equal.

In this example, the total value of the vans—$300,000—represents an increase to the company's assets account, so the accountant will debit assets for $300,000. At the same time, because the purchase was made on credit, the outflow of cash to purchase the new asset will be shown as an increased liability by crediting the accounts payable account for $300,000. Thus, although the debit and credit were applied to different accounts, the total amount of debits and credits for this transaction is equal—$300,000 for each.

The General Journal

The next question is, "Where are all these double-entry account transactions recorded?" The answer is that there are two places where business transactions are recorded—the general journal and the general ledger.

To begin, a general journal is sometimes referred to as the book of original entry because the journal is where the bookkeeper will record every daily transaction before the accountant processes the transaction information to produce financial reports. The next section discusses general ledgers in more detail, but suffice it to say here that the accountant depends on the journals as the source of information that is transferred into the ledger.

There is one very important fundamental difference between the journal and the leger — transactions in a journal are recorded chronologically, with every page organized into columns featuring transaction dates, serial numbers, transaction descriptions, account names, and debit and credit amounts.

Some companies will maintain specialized journals — for example to record only credit sales. These journals are usually created to assist in the efficiency of recording high-volume transactions. This section will limit the discussion to general journals.

A general journal may be used to record a wide variety of transactions, including asset sales, interest income, interest expense, cash or credit sales to customers, or operating expenses. To provide an illustration of how journals are used to record transactions, we'll construct an example.

- On February 3, a company purchases $2,500 in office supplies using the company credit card.
- On February 4, the company makes a credit sale of $3,750 to one customer and a cash sale of $4,250 to another customer.
- On February 5, the company ships the orders to both customers.

- On February 6, the company receives payment for the credit sale of February 4 and sends a check to the bank for the balance of the credit card bill.

Here is how the accounts might be recorded in a journal:

ABC Company Journal for 20YY			
Date	Account	Debit	Credit
03-Feb-20YY	130 Supplies Inventory	2,500	
	200 Accounts payable		2,500
04-Feb-20YY	105 Accounts Receivable	3,750	
	405 Sales Revenue		3,750
04-Feb-20YY	101 Cash	4,250	

	405 Sales Revenue		4,250
05-Feb-20YY	505 Cost of Goods Sold	8,000	
	120 Product Inventory		8,000
06-Feb-20YY	101 Cash	3,750	
	105 Accounts Receivable		3,750
06-Feb-20YY	200 Accounts Payable	2,500	
	101 Cash		2,500

Notice several important aspects of these journal entries:

- All transactions are listed chronologically
- Every debit entry is paired with a matching credit entry

- Debits are listed on the left; credits are listed on the right
- The sum of all the debit entries equals the sum of all the credit entries

These transaction entries represent bookkeeping — the first step of the accounting cycle. Although they are an invaluable record of the company's financial activity, the journal entries themselves are unhelpful in determining whether the company is generating a profit or any of the other insights for which financial statements are created. For this reason, the accountant must transfer the journal entries must be transferred into the general ledger. The next section discusses how to record entries in the general ledger.

The General Ledger

Unlike transaction records in journals that are recorded by date, transaction records in the general ledger are recorded by account. Another difference is that journal entire are entered across a page, from left to right. A standard, GAAP-compliant ledger entry uses a "T-account" format, which you can see in the following diagram. (In accounting, Dr. is the established method of abbreviating "debit; and Cr. is the established method of abbreviating "credit.")

Dr.			Cash Account		Cr.
Date	Description	Amount	Date	Description	Amount

The general ledger is the complete record of all accounts and transactions of a company. There will be a ledger page for every account listed in the chart of accounts. Many types of ledgers are available — loose-leaf binders, bound volumes, and electronic databases within computer programs.

Each specific account within a ledger will belong to one of several main categories. In addition, each of those categories is normally assigned a range of numbers, which can be used to numerically identify each of the accounts within each category. Accounts are usually are arranged in the following order:

- Assets (100-199)
- Liabilities (200-299)
- Equity (300-399)

- Revenues (400-499)
- Expenses (500-599)

Using the sample journal entries in the previous illustration, you can see that the cash account, accounts receivable, product inventory, and supplies inventory have been assigned account numbers 101, 105, 120 and 130, respectively, which make them all asset accounts. Accounts payable has been assigned account number 200, which makes it a liability account, and sales revenue has been assigned account number 405, which makes it a revenue account and cost of goods sold has been assigned account number 505, which makes it an expense account.

After the bookkeeper has entered all the daily transactions for a business into the journal, the accountant will post those transactions to the appropriate account within the ledger. The accounting term for recording transactions in ledger is "posting." Generally, accountants will post accounts from the journal to the ledger at specified time intervals, usually at the end of every month.

At the end of the accounting cycle, the accountant will total all the debits and credits in the ledger and transfer them to the trial balance.

The next section discusses the trial balance in greater detail, so for now we will use an example to illustrate how journal entries are transactions are posted to a ledger. We'll use the six journal entries from the example in the previous section to show how journal entries are posted to ledger accounts. In the following examples, each of the accounts listed in the journal entries represents an individual ledger account. Each ledger accounts starts with an opening balance on the first day of the month. As entries are posted to the ledger account from the journal, the balance is either increased or decreased. Notice that some types of accounts normally carry a debit balance; others normally carry a credit balance. Refer to the chart in the Debits and Credits section to see the effect of debit entries and credit entries on each account type.

Acct. 101		Cash		
Date		Debits	Credits	Dr. Balance
01-Feb-20YY				2,000
04- Feb-20YY		4,250		6,250

06- Feb- 20YY	3,750	2,500	7,500

Acct. 105	Accounts Receivable		
Date	Debits	Credits	Dr. Balance
01-Feb-20YY			2,500
04- Feb-20YY	3,750		6,250
06- Feb-20YY		3,750	2,500

Acct. 120		Product Inventory		
Date		Debits	Credits	Dr. Balance
01-Feb-20YY				50,000
05- Feb-20YY			5,000	45,000

Acct. 130		Supplies Inventory		
Date		Debits	Credits	Dr. Balance
01-Feb-20YY				10,000
03- Feb-20YY		2,500		12,500

Acct. 200		Accounts Payable		
Date		Debits	Credits	Cr. Balance
01-Feb-20YY				1,200
03- Feb-20YY			2,500	3,700
06-Feb-20YY		2,500		1,200

Acct. 405		Sales Revenue		
Date		Debits	Credits	Cr. Balance
01-Feb-20YY				38,000
04- Feb-20YY			3,750	41,750

04-Feb-20YY		4,250	46,000

Acct. 505		Cost of Goods Sold		
Date		Debits	Credits	Dr. Balance
01-Feb-20YY				15,000
05- Feb-20YY		8,000		23,000

Notice several important aspects of these ledger entries:

- All transactions are organized by account first, then chronologically
- Account balances are updated with every entry
- Debits are listed on the left; credits are listed on the right
- The sum of all the debit entries equals the sum of all the credit entries

At the end of the accounting cycle or reporting period, the accountant will transfer all the debit and credit totals for all the accounts in the ledger to the trial balance worksheet. The next section discusses this process in more detail.

The Trial Balance

Chapter 1 discussed the six steps of the accounting cycle:

1. Analyzing and recording transactions
2. Posting transactions to the ledger
3. Preparing a trial balance
4. Preparing adjusting entries
5. Preparing an adjusted trial balance
6. Preparing financial statements

So far, this chapter has discussed the first two steps in detail: recording transactions in the journal and posting journal entries to the ledger. This section focuses on Step 3: preparing a trial balance. The trial balance was developed as a method for allowing the accountant to check for errors in the ledger and/or the journal before preparing financial statements. (Steps 4 and 5 provide a means for correcting any errors; and the last step is the creation of the statements themselves.)

The trial balance is not only one of the most important steps of the accounting cycle; it also highlights the true value of the double-entry system of accounting. Specifically, by providing a very direct method of comparing the total credits to the total debits entered into the account ledger for any given accounting period, the trial balance allows the accountant to spit potential errors that may have occurred either when the bookkeeper recorded transactions in the journal or when those entries were posted to the ledger.

Generally, accounting software is more effective at preventing errors before this stage than manual accounting because accounting software utilizes error-checking throughout the entire process of recording transactions. In addition, the trial balance is not the only method that an accountant should use to check for errors. This section will discuss error-checking after we examine a sample trial balance.

To create trial balance worksheet, the accountant must:

1. transfer all of the accounts from the chart of accounts to the trial balance worksheet;

2. transfer the closing debit or credit balances from each account in the ledger to the appropriate account on the trial balance worksheet;

3. total all of the debt balances and all of the credit balances.

Then, if the totals of the debit balances and credit balances are the same, the books are balanced, and the accountant can move to the next step.

But first, there are three important points to remember:

1. The following types of accounts normally carry debit balances:

   a. Asset accounts

   b. Expenses accounts

2. The following types of accounts normally carry credit balances:

   a. Liability accounts

   b. Equity accounts

   c. Revenue accounts

3. The trial balance does require the accountant to add every single debt and credit for every type of account; instead, the trial balance includes the closing balances for each account as listed in the account ledger.

The following example of a trial balance worksheet uses the same example from the previous two sections. Seven of the accounts were used specifically in the examples in the previous 2 sections. Some additional accounts have been added for illustration purposes. It is possible for an accountant to include closing balances for accounts in which there were no recorded transactions during the accounting period. Every company's chart of accounts is different. This example illustrates that all of a company's accounts will be included on the trial balance worksheet, not just those for which transactions have been recorded.

Account Number	Account for ABC Company Fiscal Year 20YY	Debit Balance	Credit Balance
Asset Accounts			
101	Cash	7,500	
105	Accounts Receivable	2,500	
120	Product Inventory	45,000	
103	Supplies Inventory	12,500	

Liability Accounts			
200	**Accounts Payable**		**1,200**
205	Payroll Payable		5,250
Equity Accounts			
301	Owner's capital		20,000
320	Retained earnings		13,000
Revenue Accounts			
405	**Sales Revenue**		**46,000**
410	Service Sales Revenue		7,550
Expense Accounts			
505	**Cost of Goods Sold**	**23,000**	
510		2,500	
	Totals	93,000	93,000

Using the trial balance to check for errors

In this example, the closing balances of all accounts are equal. Notice that the closing accounts of the accounts in bold are transferred directly from the closing balances in the sample ledger entries in the previous section. The closing balances will reflect the difference to the opening balance resulting from the sum of all debits and credits posted to that account, so there is no reason for the accountant to add all the debits and credits individually.

If the totals at the bottom of the debt and credit columns do not match, there may be several reasons, including:

- An account balance may appear on the trial balance worksheet as a debit balance when it should be a credit balance (or vice-versa).
- The account balances may be incorrect as a result of a transposition error in one or more of the account balances figures.
- A debit or credit balance from one single account may have been omitted.

However, the trial balance may not detect certain types of accounting errors, such as:

- Incorrect values for debit or credit balances that do not result in unequal debt and credit balance totals.

- Transactions that were not entered into the journal.
- A transaction may have been entered as a credit, when it should have been entered as a debit.
- A transaction may have been posted to the wrong type of account.
- Two errors that offset each other may escape detection using only the trial balance worksheet.

A company's annual report and financial statements will be released to shareholders, tax authorities, financial regulators, bond and credit rating forms, and lenders. These statements may also require passage of an examination by auditors. As a result, accuracy in reporting accounting figures is vitally important to the ongoing success of a company's operations. Thus, regardless of whether the accounting error is purely mathematical or the result of more serious or complicated problems during the accounting cycle, creating the trial balance is a very important part of accurate accounting.

Chapter 7: Cash Accounting vs.

Accrual Accounting

Figure 20: Free Image

The previous chapter noted the difference between single-entry and double-entry accounting. This chapter discusses another pair of comparable accounting methods — cash-based accounting and accrual accounting. The primary difference between these two methods consists entirely in when the funds involved in a transaction are recorded. When using cash accounting, transactions are recorded when they are paid for. When using the accrual method, transactions are corded at the time the transaction occurs, regardless of whether they are paid for at that time or later. There are many reasons a business would choose one accounting method over another. Generally, smaller businesses and individuals keeping track of their personal finances use cash accounting, while businesses with a larger volume of transactions and more complex operations use accrual accounting. Each method has particular strengths and weaknesses and in any given situation, one method may be preferable to another.

This chapter discusses in detail the fundamental differences between these two accounting methods. It also discusses how some expenses may be reported differently when using one method versus the other, and how that can affect a company's financial statements.

The Cash Method

Cash accounting recognizes revenue only when cash is received and expenses only when they are paid. As a result, a cash accounting system will not use accounts payable or accounts receivable accounts. Many small businesses may use a cash accounting system for a variety of reasons:

- Cash accounting allows for the implementation of a simple and easy to use accounting and bookkeeping system.

- Small companies that do not have to submit financial statements to the SEC or to shareholders may not require a more complex system of bookkeeping and accounting.

- Using a cash accounting system makes it easier to determine whether a payment has been received or paid by simply confirming whether the money has either been deposited or withdrawn from the bank. There is no need to review invoices and accounts payable to track outstanding bills or pending payments.

- Using a cash accounting system allows for a very straightforward method of establishing the value of a company's cash account by simply checking the current bank balance.

- Companies that employ cash accounting do not have to pay taxes of revenue they have not yet received.

The Accrual Method

Accrual accounting recognizes revenue when it is earned and expenses when they are incurred, regardless of when the money is either deposited in or withdrawn from the bank. For example, let's say a customer buys a service contract from a company, and the company completes the service agreements and sends the customer an invoice. Although the customer doesn't pay the invoice for 30 days, the company records the income as revenue at the time the contract is signed. Similarly, if a company buys $2,000 in office supplies using the company credit card, the expense is recorded at the time of purchase, even if the bill isn't paid for another 30 days or longer.

The accrual method is a more common accounting method for several reasons. Primarily, the accrual method provides the company with a means to more accurately assess its income and expenses over time. Whereas the cash method allows any company to determine its cash on hand simply be checking the bank balance, the accrual method allows company to add in revenue it has earned but not received and subtract expenses it has or will incur but has not yet paid. As a result using accrual accounting can be beneficial to budget planning and essential when compiling financial statements. However, accrual accounting can also convey a false impression of profitability if it relies too heavily on accounts receivable and not enough on the value of its cash accounts. This inability to gauge cash flow can have serious consequences if a company incurs too many expenses without having the cash to pay for them.

The following chart summarizes the advantages and disadvantages of both accounting methods.

Cash Method	Accrual Method
Recognizes revenue only when cash is received	Recognizes revenue at the time it is earned, regardless of when goods and services

	are paid for.
Recognizes expenses only when cash leaves the bank.	Recognizes expenses at the time they are incurred, regardless of when they are paid for.
Cash revenue that has not yet been received cannot be taxed.	All revenue (including accounts payable) is taxable in the reporting period in which it was earned.
More common among small businesses that do not maintain a sales inventory.	Required for all businesses that generate $5 million or more.

Examples of Cash vs. Accrual Accounting

This section provides real-world examples of how cash accounting methods differ from accrual accounting methods using two specific types of transactions: prepaid expenses and unearned revenue.

- Let's say Company XYZ rents a manufacturing facility where it manufactures and sells goods to retail customers. The company pays $1,000 per month to rent its manufacturing facility.

- On December 2, the company manager receives the rental invoice for the upcoming month of January.

- The company manager signed a one-year lease agreement with the property manager.

- On December 3, the manager decides to pay all the rent for the upcoming year in one lump sum and sends a check for $12,000 to the property manager. The property manager cashes the check the same day.

- On December 7, the company receives two orders—one for $8,000 worth of goods, the other for $4,000 worth of goods. Both customers sent payment in full with their order requests.

- On December 7, the company deposits the payments for both orders into the company checking account.

- On December 8, the company delivers the first order for $4,000.

- The second order requires additional manufacturing and will not be ready for shipment until January 5.

Now, we will examine how these transactions will be recorded using both the cash method and the accrual method.

Prepaid Expenses

Company ABC pays $12,000 per year in rent to do business out of its facility. In this case, the manager paid all the rent for the following year (2020) in December 2019. Using the cash accounting method, he will record a transaction in the daily journal for the month of December for $12,000.

Using the accrual method, he will be able to take advantage of the matching principle, which allows him to allocate prepaid expenses over time. In this case, although he paid $12,000 in the month of December, he will not record any of those funds as a rental expense for December. Instead, he will record $1,000 in the general journal for each month of the upcoming year; those entries will be posted to the Rental Expense account in the general ledger, again for each month of the upcoming year.

The difference in accounting methods for prepaid expenses can affect a company's financial statement dramatically.

Using the cash method, this company's balance sheet will show a $12,000 expense for the month of December. In addition, this amount must be deducted from their annual revenue. Although the larger deduction for rent in December may allow them to pay less in taxes, their cash flow statement will not reflect an accurate picture because all of the rent for the year 2020 will have appeared on the cash flow statement for 2019, and monthly expenses for 2020 will not reflect rental expenses because the money changed hands in December 2019.

Using the accrual method, the company spends $12,000 in cash in December, but none of it is recorded as an expense for December because the money is used to pay rental expenses for 2020. The company will not be able to deduct the $12,000 as an expense on their taxes for 2019. However, their balance sheet and their cash flow statement will reflect their financial condition more accurately — not only will the $12,000 rental expenses be distributed evenly across all the months for the 2020 fiscal year; neither their balance statement nor their cash flow statement for 2019 will reflect the $12,000 expense.

Unearned Revenue

Company ABC received $12,000 in revenue in December for two orders. Using the cash method of accounting, all of that revenue will be recorded for the month of December and must be reported as income on their taxes. However, only $4,000 of the total amount sold has been delivered. As a result, the company must pay taxes in 2019 for income it has not yet earned; in addition, their balance sheet cannot reflect unearned income as a liability to offset the costs in labor to produce the remaining $8,000 in goods. As a result, it will reflect assets it has not yet earned, resulting in an inaccurate portrayal of their current financial condition.

Using the accrual method, the company can record the $4,000 in revenue it earned in December and record the $8,000 for the second order in the Unearned Revenue account under Liabilities. The accountant can also enter the amount of material and labor required to produce and ship the send order by crediting the supplies inventory and debiting the wages payable accounts. As a result, the company can defer taxation for the $8,000 in unearned revenue to the following year and produce financial statements that reflect a more accurate picture of their financial condition.

Other types of transactions

Because every transaction is different and may involve many different types of accounts, the specific differences, advantages, and disadvantages between recording those accounts using either the cash or accrual method may vary widely. However, the IRS requires that all businesses indicate withtype of accounting method they are suing. Changing accounting methods requires that the company file Form 3115.

Chapter 8: Depreciation of Fixed Assets

Everyone is familiar with the concept that when you buy a brand new car, it loses several thousand dollars in value as soon as you drive it off the dealer's lot. This decline in value is known as depreciation. Depreciation is also an accounting method that can help businesses mitigate the cost of major investments by reporting the amount of value of their fixed assets lose over time. Not all assets should be depreciated—for example, even though the new recycle bin you purchased for your office will be around for a long time, its relatively low cost make the prospect of depreciating it more trouble than it would be worth. However, major purchases such as office equipment, computers, manufacturing equipment, buildings, vehicles, and storage facilities will definitely require a major investment of capital. Using GAAP-compliant methods of depreciation, a business can deduct the cost of purchasing the asset accurately. By using this opportunity to report the purchase as a business expense, a company can reduce its taxable income, resulting in a lower tax bill, which can compensate for the initial cost of purchasing the asset.

There are specific rules governing the use of depreciation. There are also several different types of depreciation methods, including straight-line, declining balance, double declining balance, sum-of-the-year's digits, and units of production. This chapter first discusses straight-line depreciation in detail, with brief descriptions of the other types of depreciation. It also discusses the concepts of accumulated depreciation, salvage value, and net gain or loss on a sale.

Straight-line Depreciation

Put simply, depreciation is used to match the cost of a given fixed asset with the amount of revenue it generates, which allows a company to record revenues and expenses used to produce them together in the same accounting period in which they occur. Depreciation allows the accountant to show the gradual decline of the ability of the proportionate ability of the asset to produce the associated amount of revenue. By using depreciation, the financial statements provide a more accurate record of the company's financial condition and capacity to generate revenue.

Because it is almost impossible to directly link the exact amount of revenue generated with the cost of a fixed asset, established methods of depreciation instead utilize several standardized techniques and valuation methods to identify the asset's useful life and calculate its declining value over that period.

Straight-line depreciation is the standard method of calculating this figure. Straight-line depreciation is used when there is no established pattern of how an asset will be used over time, so it uses a basic formula that can be applied to any fixed asset used for any purpose under any conditions. Straight-line depreciation is also the easiest method, so there are fewer opportunities accounting errors. Following are the six steps used to calculate straight-line depreciation:

1. Determine the initial cost of the fixed asset to be depreciated.

2. Determine the salvage value of the asset.

3. Subtract the estimated salvage value of the asset from the purchase cost of the asset, as recorded in the ledger.

4. Determine an estimated useful life for the asset. Often, each type of fixed asset will have a standard useful life already assigned to it for

accounting purposes; this estimate should be used wherever possible.

5.   Divide the number of years of the estimated useful life into 1. This is the straight-line depreciation rate.

6.   Multiply the depreciation rate by the asset cost (less salvage value).

Step-by-step Straight-line Depreciation

The following example shows how straight-line depreciation can be used to record the expense of purchasing new fixed assets.

1.   Let's say Company ABC purchased a packaging machine for $50,000. The machine has an expected useful life of 15 years and an estimated salvage value of $10,000. The depreciation rate can be calculated as follows:

    a.   Depreciation rate $= 1/$Years of useful life

       i.   Depreciation rate $= 1/15\ 0.066$

       ii.   Depreciation rate $= 0.066$

       iii.   Depreciation rate $= 6.7\%$

b.　　　　　　　Asset cost (50,000) – Salvage value (10,000) = $40,000

c.　　　　　　　Adjusted asset cost ($40,000) x Depreciation rate (6.7%) = $2,680 per year.

2.　　　　　　　Next, to record the expense for purchasing this new fixed asset using depreciation, they do not have to record an expense of $50,000 at the time of purchase, even if they paid $50,000 cash. Instead, the company record the expense as follows:

a.　　　　　　　Record $2,680 against net income for the first year.

b.　　　　　　　Record $2,680 in depreciation expense for every following for the next 14 years.

c.　　　　　　　After15 years, sell the asset for the estimated salvage value of $10,000 and record any net gain or loss on the sale.

Accumulated Depreciation

Accumulated depreciation is an asset account that appears in a company's chart of accounts. The accumulated depreciation account is used to record the total depreciation of a fixed asset for the time it was first purchased and made available for use. Because the accumulated depreciation account is a contra account, it normally carries a credit balance even though it is an asset account. As a result, the accountant will report accumulated depreciation on the balance sheet as a reduction in the gross value of fixed assets.

Over the life of the asset, the balance of the accumulated depreciation account for an asset will increase, as the value of its depreciation is recorded each year. The amount of accumulated depreciation can be subtracted from the original purchase cost of the asset, or gross cost, to calculate the asset's carrying amount.

When the asset is sold at the end of its useful life, the balance of the accumulated depreciation account is reversed along with the original purchase price of the asset. This method of derecognition of the asset is completely removes it from the company's books to avoid retaining values for gross fixed assets and accumulated depreciation.

Using the example in the previous section, the following journal entries show how depreciation and derecognition would be recorded. First, the annual entry for depreciation of the packaging machine would be entered in the journal like this:

	Debit	Credit
Depreciation expense	2,680	
Accumulated depreciation		2680

After 15 years, the asset will be sold for the salvage value, so the following entry will be recorded to purge the accumulated depreciation account:

	Debit	Credit
Accumulated depreciation	40,200	
Fixed assets		40,200

Journal entries will be posted to the ledger and then to the trial balance at the conclusion of each accounting period prior to issuing financial statements. The next two sections discuss salvage value and net gains or losses on the sale of an asset.

Salvage Value

As discussed in previous sections, the salvage is the estimated value of an asset at the end of its estimated useful life. Some companies may have an established method of estimating the salvage value of certain asset types, and most companies have devised internal methods that accounting departments employ when calculating salvage value. Regardless of the method of calculating the salvage, it is important to establish that value at the time the asset is purchased because it will affect the annual depreciation charge and should be the same as the carrying value of the depreciated asset at the end of its useful life.

To calculate the salvage value, a company will take many factors into consideration. For instance, if a company believes a particular asset will have a long useful life and will contribute demonstrably to the company's revenue, the useful life of the asset will be much longer, and the salvage value may also be correspondingly lower. On the other hand, a company may be less optimistic about an asset's ability to contribute to revenue over time. As a result, the company may assign the asset a much shorter useful life with a much higher salvage value. Alternatively, using accelerated depreciation instead of straight-line depreciation can allow a company to deduct greater depreciation earlier in the asset's useful life prior to selling it for its estimated salvage value. Unfortunately, the largely unregulated area of salvage valuation had led some accountants to use this figure in a fraudulent manner. For example, if a fixed asset is assigned an artificially high salvage value, the annual depreciation may considerably lower, making it possible to report higher profits than were actually earned. Chapter 13 discusses fraud and ethics in greater detail.

Gain or Loss on Sale

The net gain or loss on the sale of an asset is recorded after an asset has reached the end of its useful life. Often, the salvage value will simply be the amount for which a company believes it will be able to sell the asset at the end of its useful life. In such cases, the closer amount received for selling the asset at the end of its useful life, the lower the net gain or loss will be recorded for. Either way, in deal circumstances, the income generated from the sale of an asset will be enough to compensate for the final carrying amount of the asset at the end of the depreciation period. If the company receives more than the salvage value recorded on the books, it records a net gain. If it receives less, it records a net loss.

Many companies may routinely depreciate an asset to a salvage value of $0 if they believe it will have minimal value at the end of its useful life, or if they believe its only salvage value will be a result of selling the asset for parts. In these cases, the entire purchase price of the asset is depreciated annually, and any proceeds from selling the asset at the end of its useful life are recorded as a net gain.

Chapter 9: Amortization of

Intangible Assets

Amortization is an accounting method whereby a company can show the costs associated with acquiring intangible assets. Chapter 8 discusses the process of depreciating fixed assets over time to provide a method of accounting for major purchases as business expenses. The costs associated with tangible, fixed assets such as furniture, machinery, buildings and vehicles — all physical objects that lose value as a result of normal wear and tear and usage over time — are accounted for through the use of depreciation. However, intangible assets, such as copyrights and trademarks, pose a different challenge to a company's accounting department. These assets are fundamentally different from fixed assets, so accounting for the costs associated with acquiring them also requires a different method.

There are many assets that may fall under the category of intangible assets. Accounts must also make several determinations when they are considering how to amortize an intangible asset. This chapter provides a detailed discussion of amortization, including a list of categories and types of intangible assets, how to use amortization to account for their value and some of the terms related to amortization.

What Are Intangible Assets?

Defining intangible assets can be a challenge. Although the concept itself is fairly easy to understand, in terms of accounting, additional considerations include whether the asset meets certain criteria and whether the intangible asset is eligible for amortization.

1. First, intangible assets are all assets owned by a company that are not physical objects or cannot otherwise be physically touched. The following fairly comprehensive list identifies many types of intangible assets:

- Registered trademarks
- Customer and client lists
- Franchise agreements
- Computer software copyrights

- Patents
- Brand names
- Logos
- Domain names
- Artistic assets, including photos, videos, paintings, films, and audio recordings
- Defensive assets acquired to prevent others from using it—for example, buying and registering an internet domain to prevent another company from using the same or a similar company name.
- Any other forms of intellectual property
- Business licenses
- Leasehold improvements, in which a landlord takes ownership of the improvements
- Proprietary software developed for internal use
- Goodwill, which is defined as the purchase price of a business entity that has been sold to another business entity, less the amount of the value not already assigned to specifically identified assets and liabilities that were acquired as a result of the acquisition.

2. To be considered an intangible asset, the asset must meet all the following criteria:
- It must be a non-physical asset.
- It must provide value to the company.

- Its benefit to the company must be in the form of a measurable effect, such as cost.
- The cost of preparing an intangible asset must be attributable to its intended use. For instance, when a company purchases a patent, it must be for the intended use of protecting patent rights for something the company invented.
- Intangible assets resulting from development may be recognized as intangible assets only if their use or sale generate future benefits, if the expenses attributed to the intangible asset can be measured, and if the company has enough resources to complete the development of the asset.

3. To qualify for amortization, an intangible asset must have a useful life of more than one year. In addition, although there are many assets that may be considered intangible asset, not all types of intangible assets can be amortized. For example, the following types of intangible assets may be amortized:

- Patents
- Copyrights
- Trademarks
- Intellectual Property
- Franchise rights
- Business licenses

On the other hand, the following types of intangible assets may not be amortized:

- Goodwill (except for private companies)
- Brand names
- Logos
- Publishing titles
- Customer lists

Straight-line Amortization

Amortization of intangible assets is an accounting process that allows companies to distribute the expenses associated with acquiring the asset over the projected life of the asset. In this way, amortization is similar to depreciation. An accountant may record different amortization values depending on whether the values are for corporate accounting purposes or for tax purposes — amortization for tax purposes requires costs to be distributed over a specific number of years regardless of the actual useful life of the asset.

As with depreciation, there are several established methods of amortization methods These methods include the straight-line method, the diminishing balance method, the unit of production method, the declining balance method, and the double-declining balance method. This section will focus on the straight-line method of amortization.

Amortizing an intangible asset using the straight-line method can be accomplished in four steps. To amortize an intangible asset:

1.   Determine the start date.

   Generally, the start date of an intangible asset is the date it was first purchased, acquired, or made available for use. For example:

   - The start date for patent is the date on which it was purchased or for which it was applied.
   - The start date of a copyright is the date it was issued.
   - The start date of a business license is the date it was obtained.

2.   Determine the initial cost of the intangible asset.

Generally, this will simply be the amount of money spent to acquire the asset. For example if a patent application required a $75,000 purchase fee, then $75,000 is the initial cost of the intangible asset. The costs required to develop the invention cannot be included.

Intangible assets that are initially developed internally, such as software developments and leasehold improvements, should be recognized at their actual cost. Any other intangible assets that are developed internally should be charged to expense in the period in which the expense is incurred.

3.   Calculate the estimated useful life of the asset.

We'll use the same example as in the previous step. If the patent purchased by the company for $75,000 protects the invention for 20 years, then this is the useful life of the intangible asset.

4.   Calculate the amortization.

The formula for calculating straight-line amortization is:

Initial Cost/Useful Life = Annual Amortization Value

Using the same example of the $75,000 patent, the amortization value will be calculated as follows:

$75,000/20=\$3750$

Legal Life vs. Expected Useful Life

One of the fundamental differences between intangible assets and fixed assets is that fixed assets typically have salvage value. The corresponding terms for salvage value as applied to intangible assets is residual value. But most intangible assets generally do not have any residual value — their entire cost can be amortized. The previous example of the patent originally had an expected useful life of 20 years; in this case, this may be expressed as its legal life, since it expires legally after the initial 20-year period of protection.

Although intangible assets rarely have residual value, it is usually advisable to conduct impairment testing to determine whether the intangible asset's carrying value may become unrecoverable — that is, if the legal or expected useful life of the intangible asset is shortened considerably, resulting in the need to write off the remaining value of the amortization. The useful life of an intangible asset may change over time. Using the example above, the 20-year patent may protect a technological invention. However, if new technology renders the invention obsolete in ten years, the useful life of the patent expires early, and the remaining value may be written off.

Other changes that may reduce or annul the legal or expected useful life of an intangible asset include:

- A significant decrease in the market price of the asset

- Any significant adverse change in the manner in which the asset is used, which damages or lessens its value

- Any significant adverse change in either the legal factors or the controlling business climate that govern the use of the asset

- Any unexpected and excessive costs incurred by the company during the process of acquiring or developing the asset

- Any operating or cash flow losses associated with the asset

- Any use of the asset that results in a likelihood of greater than 50% that it will be sold or otherwise disposed of before the end of its estimated useful life

In any of these cases, the accountant must recognize an impairment loss by debiting an impairment loss account and crediting the intangible assets account. The new carrying amount of the intangible asset will be it most recent carrying amount, less the amount of the impairment loss. In addition, amortization for the remainder of the intangible asset's expected useful life may have to be recalculated using the remaining useful life and any change to the value of the asset itself.

Chapter 10: Inventory and Cost of Goods Sold (CoGS)

For retail businesses, the inventory is likely its most important asset. A retail business generates revenue mainly be selling products to customers. While there are many other assets a retail business may depend on — its point-of-sale machines and cash registers, the facilities and buildings where its stores are housed, storage facilities, shipping materials, and in-store displays — without merchandise to sell, there would be no business to conduct.

Closely related to inventory is the Cost of Goods Sold (CoGS). Whereas inventory is an asset, CoGS is an expense. Many businesses simply buy merchandise from wholesalers and manufacturers, then sell it to retail customers. Other businesses buy the raw materials from suppliers, manufacture their inventory from the raw materials, then sell the end products to retail consumers through their stores.

Regardless of the specific details of the business model, inventory and CoGS may be the largest and most important asset and expense, respectively, of any retail business. These two financial concerns are also closely related in terms of reporting performance on financial statements. This chapter discusses in detail how to account for both inventory and CoGS, including the perpetual method, the periodic method and how to calculate to CoGS.

Inventory

Depending on the type and size of any given business, ordering and maintaining inventory can be a key aspect of that business's success. Any business that relies on the sale of merchandise as its main source of revenue must have an inventory of items readily available for its customers to purchase. A company must first purchase inventory from the wholesaler or manufacturer. This purchase is recorded as an expense known as Cost of Goods Sold. Once the inventory items have been received, they are recorded as an asset. Inventory is considered an asset on the balance sheet of a business, and they can only be expensed as they are sold to customers.

A business will indicate its beginning inventory on its income statement. Beginning inventory is the value of all the inventory that is left over from the previous year. As the new fiscal year begins, additional inventory purchases are added to this balance. At the end of the year, the value of all the products that were not sold are subtracted from the beginning inventory plus the value of any additional purchases. The result ids the Cost of Goods Sold (CoGS). This chapter discusses CoGS in the final section, but the intimal focus is on inventory.

The importance of accounting for inventory cannot be stressed enough. Inventory is reported as an asset of the balance sheet, but unlike may fixed assets or financial assets like cash or securities, inventory must be very closely monitored. A business that has too much inventory may encounter cash flow problems if they spent too much on purchasing items for resale. They may also run into additional expenses, such as storage and insurance. They can also encounter losses if the inventory becomes obsolete. On the other hand, a company that has too little inventory may lose revenue from lost sales. Because of the importance of inventory to the success of a retail business, the accounting profession has established specific methods for recording and managing inventory.

Perpetual Method

The perpetual method is a more sophisticated and far more widely used method of recording inventory. The perpetual method is more expensive than the periodic method, mostly because it requires the use of extensive technology and staff to maintain. The perpetual system is so-named because it keeps track of inventory balances of all inventory items on a continual, ongoing basis. When new inventory items are purchased by the business, they are entered into the company's computer system. As items are sold throughout the day, the company's accounting software records the sale of the item and automatically updates the inventory balance. Assuming there is no theft or damage, and assuming there is no human error regarding data input into the computerized inventory tracking software, a perpetual inventory account balance should reflect an accurate, real-time balance of any item and of all items included in the business's inventory.

To understand what a perpetual inventory system looks like in action, consider purchasing items at a grocery store. When scanned at the cash register during checkout, the barcode stamped on the item not only tell the customer and the clerk how much the items costs, but also instantly updates that total in the inventory account balances.

Especially in the modern business environment, a perpetual inventory system is a must for large businesses with high sales volumes, particularly if the business operates as a chain with many franchises in many locations. A perpetual inventory system allows these types of businesses offers advantages, such as checking for errors related to inventory, providing a comprehensive list of all transactions down the level of individual items sold. Managers can also make more informed decisions about purchasing and can more easily identify problems related to theft.

However, due to their complexity and cost, perpetual inventory systems are not right for every type of business.

Periodic Method

The periodic method of inventory requires an occasional physical count of all inventory items. Physical counts are compared against beginning inventory values to measure the relative value of existing inventory, CoGS, and what types of purchases are required to bring inventory counts to desired levels.

Business owners that use the periodic method to update inventory values at the end of set periods throughout the fiscal year—once a month, once every quarter, or annually. All purchases to restock inventory are recorded in the company's purchase account. After the inventory has been counted, the balances in the purchase account are transferred to the inventory account. The inventory account is adjusted at the end of each reporting period to account for ending balances.

- Using a periodic system, the CoGS is calculated using the following formulas:
- Beginning inventory + Purchases = Total cost of inventory (goods)
- Total cost of inventory - Ending inventory = Total cost of goods sold

The following table compares aspects of perpetual and periodic inventory systems:

	Perpetual Method	Periodic Method
Accounts	General ledger updates occur automatically	Account updates only occur after inventory counts
Technology	Businesses with many locations that conduct thousands of transactions a day cannot maintain physical counts of inventory. They are dependent on technology.	Simple manual recordkeeping of small inventories is still possible.
CoGS	Account balances are continuously	The value is calculated at the end of the

	and automatically updated as each sale is recorded.	reporting period using the formula shown above.
Cycle counting	Cycle counts can be automatically generated.	Cycle counts are not possible because inventory is not tracked in real time.
Purchases	New inventory purchases are automatically recorded and accounts balances are automatically updated.	All purchases are recorded into the purchase account manually.
Error-checking	Error checking is fairly easy by configuring search	Error checking is extremely difficult, because unit-

	parameters suing the software.	level tracking is not employed in the periodic system.

Calculating Cost of Goods Sold

The Cost of Goods Sold (CoGS) is closely related to inventory. Whereas inventory is recorded as an asset on a company's balance sheet, CoGSis reported as an expense. Depending on the type of business, CoGS may include several costs:

- For retailers that purchase items wholesale, the CoGS will include the entire purchase price the business paid to the supplier.
- For businesses that manufacture goods for sale, CoGs will include the cost of purchasing the raw materials needed to manufacture the items.
- CoGS may also include all the costs associated with preparing items for sale to customers, such as shipping, labor, manufacturing overhead, etc.

The following formula is used to calculate the CoGS:

- CoGS = Beginning Inventory + P – Ending Inventory

(P indicates purchases during the accounting cycle.) CoGS is an important part of a company's financial statements. A company's gross profits are determined by subtracting the COGS from revenue. Gross profits, in turn, provide an indication of a company's profitability. When a company's CoGS increases, its net income will decrease and understanding this relationship is useful for inventors and financial regulators.

CoGS Methods

As there are different methods of recording inventory balances, so there are different methods of calculating CoGS. The value of CoGS depends upon the method used by the business. There are three methods a company may use when recording inventory levels to arrive a t a value of CoGS: First In, First Out; Last In, Last Out (LIFO); and the Average Cost method.

- **First-In First-Out Method (FIFO)**

Using this method, the inventory goods that were purchased earliest are sold first. Generally, prices for all goods tend to increase over time, so companies using FIFO will sell items for which it paid a lower price first. Bey selling its least expensive items first, the CoGs for the reporting period will be lower, resulting in a higher net income over time.

- **Last-In First-Out Method (LIFO)**

Using this inventory method, the inventory items that a company purchased at the latest date are sold first. Again, because the cost of most items tends to increase over time, calculating CoGS according to this method generally results in higher CoGS value at the end of the reporting period, thereby resulting in a lower reported net income.

• Average Cost Method

Finally, the Average cost method simply averages the purchase cost of all of the same type of items currently held in a company's inventory, regardless of purchase date. This method generally cancels out changes in the purchase price of inventory items over time. As a result, the CoGS figure is not as heavily impacted by significant costs related to a single purchase or series of purchases. Net income figures are much more stable when using this system.

Chapter 11: Budgeting for Your Business

Figure 21: Free Image

If you have ever been responsible for paying any kind of bill for any kind of household expense, you have at least some experience in budgeting. Usually, whenever someone receives a bill for a credit card or other service, such as gas, electricity or telephone, the first question that runs through your mind is, "Do I have enough money to pay this bill?" After thinking about the balance in your checking account, other bills you may have recently received, and any events you may have planned for the weekend, you'll answer either yes or no. If your answer is no, you will likely begin thinking of ways to come up with money to pay the bill. This aspect of money management is part of budgeting, although this example illustrates budgeting practices that are far from ideal.

Business budgeting is the practice of considers all the time, money and resources available, then formulating a plan for how to manage operations in such a way as to use all available resources to a maximum advantage. Depending on the size and complexity of your business, the amount of resources available to you, the current economic climate and your goals and objectives for growth, the budgeting process can range from routine and relatively straightforward to arduous, painstaking and extremely challenging. Regardless, running a business without some type of budget is not a good practice. Fortunately, established business using professional accounting practices have developed many standardized forms of business budgeting, so you will not have to completely invent a process from scratch. This chapter discusses many of the complexities of professional commercial budgeting, including a general overview, budget planning and control, the advantages of budgeting and the many different types of budgets.

What is Budgeting?

In simple terms, a budget is a financial plan for future activities. Whereas, your home budget may include allocations of money for vacation, utilities, mortgage or rent, and groceries, a business budget will be concerned with such priorities as production, inventory, sales and capital expenditures.

A well-designed budget can help a business decide which areas of growth it will pursue, and what resources it will use to do so. In addition, a budget can be an indispensable yardstick when compared to a balance sheet and can help a business determine how well it managed to stay on course with its plans for revenue and growth.

Alternatively, a budget can help businesses that are experiencing slow growth or expenses that seem too high find ways to trim spending and reallocate resources in an effort to return operations to a more profitable path. By identifying variances — i.e., differences between actual expenditures and budgeted costs — managers can pinpoint where resources may need to be reined in.

Regardless of the type of budget, all of them will likely share four basic characteristics:

1. Show management's specific plans for the coming fiscal periods;

2.   Provide specific numeric allocations of resources for achieving those goals;

3.   Require all levels of management to engage actively in conscious debate and decision-making about the direction of the company;

4.   Motivate management and staff toward achieving the goals in the budget.

Planning and Control

- ### Planning

Planning and control are two fundamental aspects of the budget process. Every budget is, by definition, a plan. Depending on the size and complexity of a business, the resources it may have available for use, and the current economic climate, a budget planning session may range anywhere from very simple to extremely complex.

This chapter discusses the many types of budgets that are in wide use in a later section. However, most budget plans will include at the very least a projected income statement with forecasts for expected growth. More complex budget planning may include considerations for the specific components and division of a company's operations, including sales forecasts, inventory purchases, fixed asset purchases. Still others will even include detailed cash flow statements indicating exactly how retained earnings should be spent, how much should be allocated for investing in new equipment and an estimate of how much financing may be required.

The larger and more complex the organization, the greater number of budget and the more details should be included in each one. In cases where organizations require several budgets to cover all areas of operations, the company should also create a master budget that contains a summary of all budgeting items, with details for individual components more specific departments.

Budgets can also vary in terms of the length of time for which they will be in effect. There are drawbacks to using long-term budgets because no budget, regardless of how thorough, can ever account for every possible change or event. In such cases, intermittent budget planning meetings may be required to make updates and adjustments to existing budgets.

Many companies simply use electronic spreadsheet software, like Microsoft Excel, to compose, post, and distribute budgets. Most software of this type is sufficiently powerful to handle even complex mathematical formulas for creating accurate projections of costs and revenue. However, may companies will purchase software designed specifically for creating budgets. There may be a variety of reasons for choosing such applications, including automatic error-checking, a lower possibility of mathematical errors, ease of use, or specific functions that enable budgeting for extremely complex or highly specialized financing needs.

A primary reason many organizations hold budget planning session is to establish a baseline against which the company can measure its future performance. This use of a budget may require frequent updates to account for unforeseen changes, but any adjustments to the budget should be made to ensure the comparison to the original baseline is as accurate as possible, rather than to retro-fit actual results to reflect an artificially optimistic comparison to the baseline.

• Control

Although budget planning is an indispensable step in the eventual creation of a usable budget, without effective controls most budgets will likely remain nothing more than a detailed list of intentions and aspirations. If budget planning can be compared to mapping out a travel route, budget controls represent the tools and agreed methods the navigator will use during the journey to ensure a safe arrival.

Once the budget has been issued, budgetary controls are used to ensure that all spending, purchasing, and management decisions are made in an effort to realize the goals stated in the budget. Management may employ many techniques throughout any given fiscal cycle to monitor progress throughout the period. When deviations and variances are detected, management will have the knowledge to step in and make changes to restore business activity to the plan of action laid out in the budget.

Performance measure controls

Consider the enormous array of resources available to an accounting department — particularly an accounting department that utilizes accounting software — to assess any division of a company's operations. By using the established principles of accounting and well-kept records, an accountant can make a determination at any given time exactly how well a company has maintained adherence to objective established in the budget.

- By periodically checking budgeted amounts for sales revenues with current balances, the company can pinpoint bottlenecks to find where inefficiencies or business failures may be occurring.
- By reviewing budget models for part of sales or manufacturing processes that are costing value, budgeting controls can ensure that necessary expenditures are allocated to accommodate increased volume.
- Using the final budget model for performance appraisals can improve motivation among staff to reach goals.
- Creating separate budgets for all responsible parties can increase the sense of autonomy and also improve motivation.

Accuracy and error-checking

Budgeting controls can also be implemented during the planning stages to ensure budgets are created with maximum efficiency and clarity and a minimum of errors. For example:

- By creating budgets for groups of employees, companies can dramatically reduce the number of line items in a budget.

- Managers may be more likely to make errors in budget models, so requesting that accountants design pre-filled templates can cut costs associated with revisions.

- Manually checking budgets for errors, with a final round of budget reviews by the entire budget planning team everyone can help companies avoid long-term losses.

- Using all available security measures to ensure the final budget is protected from unauthorized access.

- Using tracking logs can make meetings to discuss changes to the budget effective and more efficient.

Advantages of Budgeting

Some companies choose to operate without a budget to avoid the costs and frustrations of complex budget planning sessions. Operating without a budget can be risky and requires ongoing short-term forecasts to ensure the company has enough cash to continue paying its bills and fund operations. With enough discipline and attention, operating without a budget can be an effective method of management. However, most businesses find that having a budget in place is a more advantageous method of managing operations. Following are five specific advantages to maintaining an operation budget:

1. Businesses can coordinate their activities more effectively.

2. Managers have better awareness of the operating plans for other managers in other departments.

3. Employees who are made aware of the specific details of budget see themselves as a more integral part of the business and become more highly motivated and more conscious about their use of resources.

4. A budget provides a company with a concrete method for reviewing its organizational

plans, which makes implementing changes more feasible and increases the likelihood that they will lead to success.

5.   Managers who participate in budget planning will be inspired to foster a vision for the company that may otherwise have gone unnoticed or undiscovered.

Different Types of Budgets

Most of this chapter has discussed budgets in general terms. To some degree it is necessary to discuss budgeting in general terms because the specific goals, needs, and resources of any business will be vastly different from every other business. Budgets, too, will be similarly unique, so trying to provide universally applicable budget templates does not serve any practical purpose.

However, this section will provide a brief overview of the many types of budgets most businesses use throughout the accounting cycle.

To begin, most companies will formulate two types of budgets:

• operational budgets

- capital budgets

Operational budgets provide projected spending and revenue goals for all the various aspects of a company's operating activities — the core functions of the business. These types of budgets may include projected revenue, expenditures, and other allocations for any of the following operating activities:

- projections for sales revenue
- projections for production of goods
- amounts allocated to each department for expenses
- a master budget that summarizes all of the operational budgets and includes a master profit plan
- a cash budget that incorporates cash receipts and disbursements
- projected financial statements that will be compared to the financial statements issued at the end of the accounting cycle

Other types of operational budgets may include:

- materials budgets
- manufacturing budgets
- administrative cost budgets
- plant utilization budgets
- research and development budgets

In addition, any of these budgets may use any of the following budgeting styles:

- fixed or static budgets, which is not adjusted or changed over the course of the budget cycle
- flexible budgets, which allow for changes and adjustments in response to changes in volume or activity
- rolling budgets (also known as continuous or perpetual budgets) which provides management with a budget that looks ahead one full accounting cycle

After completing budget planning meetings and the approval process, operational budgets are used as the detailed roadmap for the business's operational activities in the next fiscal cycle.

Capital budgets account for activities that may not be directly related to operational activities and that may overlap several accounting cycles. Capital budgets are less concerned with the day-to-day operations of a business and focus instead on major projects and capital expenditures for fixed assets. A capital budget will generally consist of a detailed listing of each project, with the specific amounts allocated for each project and the projected revenue they are expected to generate. These types of budgets may also rank projects according to their priority and expected profitability. Capital budgets are sued as the roadmap not only for investments in fixed assets in future fiscal cycles, but also how the financing for these projects will be arranged.

Chapter 12: Important Principles

and Conventions of Accounting

Figure 22: Free Image

Chapter 5 of this book discusses the GAAP and the regulatory agencies that assume responsibility for ensuring that financial statements are issued according to established standards. Your business may use accounting software, or perhaps you have outsourced your bookkeeping and accounting responsibilities or hired a private accountant to maintain your books for you. As a result, because of the collective knowledge of agencies that enforce the GAAP and the skills of professional accounting services, you may not consider as important whether you have a firm grasp of the underlying assumptions of the accounting profession. However, making good business decisions requires the ability to interpret your company's financial statements independently and to make and follow-through on decisions based on quality financial intelligence. Even if your accountant make recommendations about budgeting and investment, that advice is only as valuable as far as you are able to understand why your accountant has made those recommendations and how implementing can help your business grow and thrive.

By taking some time to consider some of the important principles and conventions of accounting, you can become a better business manager and can help your business enter the phase of growth and prosperity you hoped for at founding. This chapter explores many of the most important fundamental accounting principles and provides an overview of many other principles and conventions.

Learning to Classify Different Accounts

Much of this book has discussed many of the methods and practices employed by professional accountants to ensure the records of business transactions they are responsible for recording are reliable and reflect an accurate picture of the company's financial condition at any given point in time, and comparatively over consecutive reporting periods. Double-entry accounting, in particular, was developed to ensure that accountants had a reliable means of checking for errors prior to closing the books and producing financial statements. Accounting software has made error-checking easier because most programs will alert users to errors as they enter data and will not accept inaccurate or unbalanced entries to journals or ledgers.

The accuracy and reliability of accounting data depends particularly on one aspect of accounting — ensuring that you have classified the income or expense correctly and have debited or credited the right type of account. Remember that there are five major types of account classifications:

Asset accounts. Asset accounts are things of value that a company owns. Using the accrual method of accounting, assets may include not only cash on hand, but accounts receivable that representative money you have already earned, but that the customer has not yet paid.

Liability accounts. These accounts to some degree are the opposite of asset accounts. Liabilities are financial obligations — bills the company owns for payments on loans or mortgages. If an account is a liability account, if often ends with the word "payable," rather than "receivables."

Owner's or shareholders' equity accounts. These accounts represent capital — cash, stock, or real estate — that offset the amount of money the company owes in liabilities. If all a company's liabilities are subtracted from its assets, the remaining value is the owner's equity — how much of the business's value that is in the owner's possession. If the company is publicly traded, these accounts are known as shareholders' equity accounts. The main account in this type of category is the Retained Earnings account. This account records the amount of sales revenue a company retinas and reinvests back in the business.

Revenue accounts. These accounts record two types of transactions — revenue resulting from operating activities, which are the core functions of any given business — and revenue resulting from non-operating activities such as investments and income from rental payments on buildings owned by the business.

Expense accounts. Any type of expenditure made to support the operating and non-operating activities of a business can be considered an expense. There may be many types of expenses accounts, such as office supplies, or utility and rental payments.

The accuracy of a company's financial records depends not only on ensuring that the amount of every transaction is recorded correctly, but that each transaction is attributed to the right type of account. For example, accounting errors will be reflected in the trial balance prior to generating financial statements if debits and credits are attributed to liability or expense accounts when they should be attributed to asset or revenue accounts. Double-entry accounting provides for very reliable and thorough financial reporting system, but only if it is used as intended. The following section provides a brief overview of many accounting principles that are essential to effective accounting and bookkeeping.

The Business Entity Principle

This accounting principle assumes that all of the transaction information recorded in journals and ledgers that eventually comprise the data in financial statements is derived exclusively from the financial activity of a recognized business entity, separate from its owners' personal financial activity, and separate from the financial activity of other business entities.

The Monetary Unit Principle

The monetary unit principle assumes that all of a company's financial activities will be expressed in terms of monetary units. Whether the accountant is measuring labor, natural resources, time, cash, or inventory, the values for those entities will be expressed in monetary terms.

The Periodicity Principle

Periodicity is an accounting concept that assumes that records of company's financial activities will be organized according to annual, quarterly, and monthly statements. To create accurate financial statements for a company, financial transactions must be identified as belonging to an identifiable financial period.

The Going Concern Principle

This accounting principle assumes that all of the business activity as reflected in the financial transaction recorded in journals and ledgers is for a business entity whose operations can be considered ongoing. In other words, the assumption made when accounting for the business's finances is that it will continue to operate as a business for an indefinite period of time into the future.

The Historical Cost Principle

This principle assumes that purchases transactions recorded in a company's books will retain the values at the time the asset was purchased. For instance, if real estate was purchased at $500,000 in 2010, that the purchase price will be retained even if the purchase price of the same real estate in 2015 is not $750,000.

The Full Disclosure Principle

This principle assumes that a company's financial statements will reveal all information that is necessary to gain an understanding of their financial condition, especially when withholding such data would result in investors forming an understanding that may be detrimental to their actions.

Generally Agree Accounting Principles (GAAP)

The GAAP are 10 principles that form the foundation of established professional accounting practices in the United States. A complete list of these principles appears in Chapter 5 of this book.

Chapter 13: Fraud and Ethics

Figure 23: Free Image

No one likes to be thought of as dishonest or potentially fraudulent in his or her business dealings, so it is often difficult to discuss the subject of fraud and ethics in accounting. Most businesses are run by honest managers and employee honest workers and staff. Regulatory agencies and the GAAP have made the profession of accounting an efficient and reliable way for professionals, investors, government agencies, financial regulators, bankers, and other shareholders to communicate with one another about important ventures and decisions that sometimes impact large segments of the world's populations.

At the same time, we have all witnessed a recent increase in the occurrence of scandals and corruption at the level of financial accounting that has caused tremendous damage throughout the global system of finance, government, and business. Unfortunately, the more skilled and talented a professional accountant becomes at recording and processing business transactions, the greater opportunities there will be for fraud and deception by hiding embezzlement, misappropriation of funds, and other financial crimes behind financial statements that appear to be legitimate. Perhaps the most famous example was the collapse of Enron Corporation and its accounting from Arthur Andersen, LLP after their efforts to lie to the SEC about their revenues, thereby defrauding their shareholders and many innocent civilians out of billions of dollars. Both corporations collapsed and many people were sent to prison.

The issue of ethics and fraud in accounting goes far beyond a philosophical discussion of right and wrong. Well-disciplined, honest accounting accompanied by due diligence is the lifeblood of the world's economy, and people's lives quite literally depend on the ability and willingness of accountants to keep clean books. This chapter discusses many of these concerns specifically, including the causes of fraud, fraud prevention techniques and how to detect fraudulent accounting on your business.

Fraud: Definition and Causes

Fraud is a deliberately deceptive or otherwise dishonest act by an individual, group, or organization that is intended to impose some type of loss on one party to the benefit of the fraudulent party. Fraud involves a form of deception that results in the victim surrendering some type of legal right, usually unknowingly and as a result of deceptive or misleading information.

There are many types of fraud that range from false claims in advertising campaigns, to political fraud involving false political promises in exchange for political favors, to occupational fraud involving improper use of company resources by employees, to tax fraud involving inaccurate financial reporting to avoid paying taxes, to accounting fraud, in which financial statements conceal of distort the financial condition of a company in order to make the look more profitable or more valuable than it actually is to gain leverage in negotiating with lenders, or to lure potential investors, or to hide wrongdoing from financial regulators.

Fraud has become a very serious and very common problem in business, particularly at the level of large, multinational corporations. In 2001. The collapse of the energy corporation Enron and its accounting form, Andersen Accounting made international headlines when top-level company executives were convicted and sent to prison for filing falsified financial statements with the SEC. During the economic collapse of 2008, many of the financial institutions that were instrumental in the founding of the United States were forced to close as a result of dishonest and fraudulent accounting and bookkeeping practices. All of the most serious financial corruption scandals have occurred since 2000.

The tragedy of financial fraud lies beyond the loss of cherished institutions and the value they bring to society. The financial scandals of 2001 and 2008 affected the lives of millions of Americas, and millions of others around the world, most of whom had no direct relations or equitable interest in Enron or any of the major banks that were forced to close their doors permanently. The profession of accountancy provides all professional accountants with the knowledge, skills, ability, and access to information and resources that require diligent and honest attention to ensure success. At the same time, all professional accountants may be in a better position than most to abuse the laws and regulations that govern the global financial system. As a professional accountant, it is not only your responsibility to balance the books before you close them, but also to watch for signs of fraud and report them immediately if you suspect criminal activity.

What You Can Do to Detect and Prevent Fraud in Your Business

Implementing internal audit controls to detect and stop fraudulent activity early is the best solution to accounting fraud. As a professional accountant, you will be licensed and qualified and in a better position than most to determine how to formulate and implement such programs of fraud detection where you work.

Fraud prevention measures may include:

- routine management reviews
- real-time data transaction analysis
- whistleblower programs
- rigorous client and partner vetting
- soft compliance strategies that discourage company cultures that reward bad behavior, such as tipster hotlines and employee interviews that include qualitative feedback

Accounting audits and workplace mechanisms can be extremely helpful in constructing paper trails to locate individual perpetrators after acts of financial corruption have occurred. However, by the time these few individuals are brought to justice, it's often too late to undo the considerable damage they may have already done. Studies have shown that the most important factor influencing the likelihood that accounting fraud will take place at any given company is whether that company supports a culture in which bad behavior is rewarded and good behavior is punished. Accounting tools should most definitely to be used to ensure that financial records are accurate and that financial statements are transparent and in compliance with all regulations regarding disclosure and due diligence. Accounting tool should also be used to conduct frequent and regular audits to detect possible signs of fraud. Where there's smoke, there's fire, and if you detect accounting irregularities that seem disproportionately large or frequent you should take immediate action—as a licensed CPA, the law requires to act in the interest of the GAAP.

But, most importantly, an ounce of prevention is worth a pound of cure, and stopping fraud before it starts the only to keep the books clean. The following organizations and publications may be helpful if you are interested in formulating a fraud prevention effort:

- AICPA Code of Professional Conduct
- The Association of Certified Fraud Officers – ACFE
- The International Ethics Standards Board for Accountants – IESBA
- Cybercrime: An Overview of the Federal Computer Fraud and Abuse Statute and Related Federal Criminal Laws
- SEC Litigation Releases
- The Alphabetical List of the Most Important Accounting Scandals Across 12 Countries and Beyond since about 1980
- Report to the Nation on Occupational Fraud and Abuse - Association of Certified Fraud Examiners (ACFE)
- PricewaterhouseCoopers Global Economic Crime Survey
- The Cost of Malicious Cyber Activity to the U.S. Economy

Chapter 14: Jobs in Accounting

When many people think about Certified Public Accountants and the accounting profession, they often conjure up an image of a boring, clerical office job crunching numbers with a calculator and spreadsheet to make sure the company has enough money to pay the bills. To be sure, maintaining a close watch on the spending and earning habits of the company whose books you keep is a large part of the accounting professions. However, as this book has shown, accounting is one of the oldest and most well-established professional fields. If anything, the need for the services of qualified accountants has only grown more urgent over time. Unlike many areas of business, in which advances in technology have resulted in a steep decline in the quality and quantity of qualified professionals, the need for highly skilled accountants is even greater now.

The field of accounting offers vast opportunities for people of every background, regardless of their interests. Financial services is the most obvious are in which an accounting degree can lead, but there are also accounting professionals employed in government and public service, as well as a wide variety of private sector enterprises ranging from entertainment and sports to law enforcement and healthcare to education and research.

A career in accounting requires a bachelor's degree and some type of licensing certification, especially for those who want to practice as a Certified Public Accountant. Following are lists of job titles available to qualified applicants at many companies and firms, organized by area:

- Government and Nonprofit Accounting:
  - Fund Accountancy
  - Internal Revenue Service Division of Accountancy
- Public Sector Accounting:
  - Cost Estimator
  - Enrolled Agent
  - Forensic Accountant
  - Real Estate Appraiser
  - Tax Accountant
  - Tax Attorney
  - Tax Preparer

- Private Sector Accounting:
  - Accounting Clerk
  - Accounts Payable/Receivable Clerk
  - Accounting Information System Specialist
  - Actuarial Accountant/Insurance Accountant
  - Bookkeeping Manager
  - Budget Analyst
  - Capital Accountant
  - Comptroller/Financial Controller
  - Cost Accountant
  - Environmental Accountant/Sustainability Measurement
  - Payroll Accountant
- Financial Services Accounting:
  - Business Valuation Specialist
  - Certified Financial Planner
  - Financial Analyst
  - Tax Consultant

Chapter 15: Glossary

Common Terms Used in Bookkeeping and Accounting

Account: An area in a ledger that is reserved for the recording of specific types of business transactions. For example, all expense transactions will be recorded in the Expenses account.

Accounting: The professional practice of posting bookkeeping records into a ledger, balancing accounts, and producing financial statements.

Accounting Cycle: The complete cycle of processing bookkeeping records, from recording transactions in journal to producing financial statements. The accounting cycle has six steps.

Accounting Equation: The basic accounting equation is Assets = Liabilities + Owners' Equity. The accounting equation is used to ensure that records in a double-entry accounting system are balanced.

Accountant: The professional practice of processing and evaluating bookkeeping records. Sometimes used interchangeably with "bookkeeper."

Accounts Payable (A/P): All records that show the amount of money a company owes for goods and services, which it has not yet paid.

Accounts Receivable (A/R): All records that show the amount of money owed to a company for goods and services, which it has not yet received.

Accrual Accounting: An accounting method that recognizes and records income and expenses at the time they are incurred, instead of at the time they are paid.

Assets: All items owned by a company that represent value to the business.

Bad Debts: Unpaid sales invoices for goods and services already sold that the company has written off as an expense.

Balance Sheet: A financial report that provides information about a company's value. The balance sheet shows the value of a company's assets, liabilities, and equity at a specific point in time. The balance sheet is one of three reports that comprise financial statements. The other two reports are the income statement and the cash flow statement.

Bookkeeper: The professional responsible for recording every daily transaction of a business in a financial journal. Sometimes used interchangeably with "accountant."

Bookkeeping: The practice of recording the details of financial business transactions in a journal.

Budget: A detailed financial plan for future business activities.

Capital: Funds or other forms of fixed assets that have been invested into a business to enable operations.

Cash Accounting: An accounting method that recognizes and records income and expenses at the time they are paid, instead of at the time they are earned or incurred.

Cash Flow: The record of how the money generated by a business is managed. Cash flow statements show how the business owners spend the money generated by operating and non-operating activities.

Chart of Accounts: A list of all the financial accounts contained in a company's general ledger. All accounts belong to one of five main categories: Assets, Liabilities, Equity, Revenue, Cost of Goods Sold, and Expenses. Each individual category contains several accounts to record specific types of transactions.

Closing Balance: The final balance of a ledger account at the end of a business day or bookkeeping or accounting cycle.

Coding: The practice of classifying transactions according to the chart of accounts.

Contra: A type of ledger account that allows accountants to counterbalance entries. For example, the Allowance for Bad Debts account is a contra account that allows accountants to resolve discrepancies in the Sales Revenue account.

Cost of Goods Sold: The money spent by a company to purchase inventory items for retail sales. This value can also refer to the cost of raw materials purchased for the manufacture of products for resale.

Credit: Accounting entries that occupy the right side of a double-entry ledger. Credits increase the value of income, liability, and equity accounts and decrease the value of asset and expense accounts.

Credit Note: A transaction record issued when money is refunded to a customer.

Creditor: Anyone who lends money or extends credit.

Data: All of the information recorded in journals and ledgers.

Debit: Accounting entries that occupy the left side of a double-entry ledger. Debits decrease the value of income, liability, and equity accounts and increase the value of asset and expense accounts.

Debtor: Anyone who borrows money.

Deductible: Any business purchase that can be recorded in the business's expense account.

Depreciation: The practice of recording the cost of purchasing fixed assets over their entire useful life.

Double-Entry: Double-entry accounting requires two entries for every transaction—a debit entry and a credit entry. Accountants must ensure that the value of all debit entries equals the value of all credit entries for every accounting cycle.

Drawing: An account that records payment of the owner's salary.

Entry/Entries: A single transaction recorded in a company's ledger.

Equity: The amount of financial interest the owner and/or shareholders have in a business. Equity is the difference between the value of assets and liabilities.

Expense: Any business purchases that support operations.

Financial Statements: Specific types of financial reports that show investors, managers, and regulators the financial health of a company. The three types of financial statements are the balance sheet, income statement, and the cash flow statement.

Fiscal Year: A period spanning 12 consecutive months and that constitutes an entire accounting cycle. A fiscal year can begin in any calendar month.

Gross Profit: The value of a business's income that remains after subtracting the cost of goods sold.

Income: All of the money earned by a business, either through the sales of goods and services, or through interest earned and investments.

Inventory: Items owned by a company that are available for sale.

Invoice: A document that provides the details of purchases, such as the goods or services purchased, the purchase date, and the purchase amount.

Journal: A chronological record of daily business transactions maintained by a bookkeeper. Also known as the book of original entry.

Ledger: The volume to which journal transactions are posted by the accountant; the permanent record of daily business transactions, organized by account type.

Liability: All of the money that a company owes.

Loan: Money given to a company or person on the condition that it will be repaid according to specified terms, usually with interest.

Loss: A financial result that occurs when expenses are greater than income. The opposite of profit.

Net Profit: The value of all money earned by a company from operating and non-operating activities, calculated by subtracting the cost of expenses from gross profit.

Opening Balance: The balance of a ledger account on the first day of a financial period.

Payable: A type of expense account that records the amount of money due to be paid by a business.

Payroll: The financial account that records all transactions related to employee wages.

Petty Cash: A financial account that records transactions for minor purchases.

Profit: A financial result that occurs when income is greater than expenses. The opposite of loss.

Purchase: The buying of goods, services, or assets.

Quote: An official estimate of the amount of the cost of goods or services.

Receipt: A document issued to a customer after a purchase that shows the details of the sale.

Receivable: A type of asset account that records the amount of money due to be paid to a business.

Reconcile: The accounting practice of matching balances from one document to another.

Recurring: Any transaction that takes place on a regular, repeating basis, such as a monthly utility bill.

Refund: Money that returned to customers as a result of a dispute, an overpayment, or some other reason.

Reimburse: A payment made to compensate for some type of loss.

Salary: A fixed, predetermined sum of money paid by an employer for an agreed period in exchange for work.

Sales: All money received as a result of goods or services purchased by customers.

Single-Entry: A method of recording transactions in which the transactions are only listed once.

Software: Any type of computer program. Accounting software includes QuickBooks, which automates many accounting tasks.

Statement: A financial report that displays information, such as a bank statement.

Transaction: Any type of business activity that requires a transfer of funds.

Transfer: The movement of monetary funds from one account to another account.

Undeposited Funds: An asset account that shows the amount of money that a company has received but has not yet been deposited into the bank.

Withdrawal: A transaction in which money is taken out of a financial account.

Write-Off: An accounting transaction that officially recognizes that a specified amount of money that is due to be paid will not be received.

Year-End: The period of financial accounting activity that occur at the end of a fiscal year.

Resources

10 Basic Accounting Principles & Key Assumptions - [2019 GAAP Guide]. (n.d.). Retrieved from https://www.myaccountingcourse.com/accounting-principles.

10 Best Jobs for Accounting Majors in 2019. (n.d.). Retrieved from https://www.zippia.com/accounting-major/.

40 Top Paying Accounting Jobs. (2019, September 27). Retrieved from https://www.accounting-degree.org/top-paying-accounting-jobs/.

About the Division of Corporation Finance. (2015, October 5). Retrieved from https://www.sec.gov/divisions/corpfin/cfabout.shtml.

About the Division of Enforcement. (2007, August 2). Retrieved from https://www.sec.gov/enforce/Article/enforce-about.html.

Accessing the U.S. Capital Markets - A Brief Overview for
Foreign Private Issuers. (2013, February 20). Retrieved
from
https://www.sec.gov/divisions/corpfin/internatl/for
eign-private-issuers-overview.shtml#IIIB1d2.

Accounting Basics - Income Statement: AccountingCoach.
(n.d.). Retrieved from
https://www.accountingcoach.com/accounting-
basics/explanation/2.

Accounting Basics: Explanation: AccountingCoach. (n.d.).
Retrieved from
https://www.accountingcoach.com/accounting-
basics/explanation.

Accounting Careers. (n.d.). Retrieved from
http://www.allaccountingcareers.com/accounting-
careers.

Accounting for Inventory and Cost of Goods Sold (COGS):
IAS 2 / ASC 330. (n.d.). Retrieved from
http://tfageeks.com/accounting-for-inventory-and-
cost-of-goods-sold-cogs-ias2-asc360/.

Accounting Jobs. (n.d.). Retrieved from

> https://www.glassdoor.com/Job/accounting-jobs-
> SRCH_KO0,10.htm.

Accounting Principles: Explanation: AccountingCoach. (n.d.).
Retrieved from

> https://www.accountingcoach.com/accounting-
> principles/explanation.

AICPA Mission and History. (n.d.). Retrieved from

> https://www.aicpa.org/about/missionandhistory.htm
> l.

Amortization of Certain Intangible Assets. (2004, December 1).
Retrieved from

> https://www.journalofaccountancy.com/issues/2004/
> dec/amortizationofcertainintangibleassets.html.

Amortization of Intangible Assets Definition and Meaning:
AccountingCoach. (n.d.). Retrieved from

> https://www.accountingcoach.com/terms/A/amortiz
> ation-of-intangible-assets.

Balance Sheet - Definition & Examples (Assets = Liabilities Equity). (n.d.). Retrieved from https://corporatefinanceinstitute.com/resources/knowledge/accounting/balance-sheet/.

Balance Sheet Liabilities: AccountingCoach. (n.d.). Retrieved from https://www.accountingcoach.com/balance-sheet/explanation/2.

Balance Sheets, Explained (With Examples): Bench Accounting. (n.d.). Retrieved from https://bench.co/blog/accounting/balance-sheet/.

Basic Accounting Principles - AccountingVerse. (n.d.). Retrieved from https://www.accountingverse.com/accounting-basics/basic-accounting-principles.html.

Basic Cash Flow Statement. (n.d.). Retrieved from https://www.khanacademy.org/economics-finance-domain/core-finance/accounting-and-financial-stateme/financial-statements-tutorial/v/basic-cash-flow-statement.

Bluest, K. (2017, November 21). Bookkeeping: Classification of Accounts. Retrieved from https://smallbusiness.chron.com/bookkeeping-classification-accounts-55421.html.

Blystone, D. (2019, September 17). Understanding Periodic Inventory vs. Perpetual Inventory. Retrieved from https://www.investopedia.com/articles/investing/053115/understanding-periodic-vs-perpetual-inventory.asp.

Bookkeeping - Balance Sheet and Income Statement are Linked: AccountingCoach. (n.d.). Retrieved from https://www.accountingcoach.com/bookkeeping/explanation/11.

Bookkeeping Terms and Basic Accounting Definitions. (n.d.). Retrieved from https://www.beginner-bookkeeping.com/bookkeeping-terms.html.

Bragg, S. (2019, September 16). The periodicity assumption. Retrieved from https://www.accountingtools.com/articles/the-periodicity-assumption.html.

Bragg, S. (2019, January 26). The difference between the periodic and perpetual inventory systems. Retrieved from https://www.accountingtools.com/articles/what-is-the-difference-between-the-periodic-and-perpetual-in.html.

Bragg, S. (2018, December 17). Trial balance: Example: Format. Retrieved from https://www.accountingtools.com/articles/2017/5/16/the-trial-balance-example-format.

Bragg, S. (2018, December 9). Balance sheet. Retrieved from https://www.accountingtools.com/articles/2017/5/11/balance-sheet.

Bragg, S. (2018, May 23). The balance sheet. Retrieved from https://www.accountingtools.com/articles/2017/5/17/the-balance-sheet.

Bragg, S. (2018, July 2). The monetary unit principle. Retrieved from https://www.accountingtools.com/articles/2017/5/15/the-monetary-unit-principle.

Bragg, S. (2018, December 27). Cost of goods sold journal entry. Retrieved from https://www.accountingtools.com/articles/2017/5/13/cost-of-goods-sold-journal-entry.

Bragg, S. (2019, January 12). The income statement. Retrieved from https://www.accountingtools.com/articles/2017/5/17/the-income-statement.

Bragg, S. (2019, August 6). What is GAAP? Retrieved from https://www.accountingtools.com/articles/what-is-gaap.html.

Bragg, S. (2019, August 1). Double entry accounting. Retrieved from https://www.accountingtools.com/articles/2017/5/17/double-entry-accounting.

Bragg, S. (2019, January 21). Cash basis vs. accrual basis accounting. Retrieved from https://www.accountingtools.com/articles/cash-basis-vs-accrual-basis-accounting.html.

Bragg, S. (2019, January 11). Accumulated depreciation. Retrieved from https://www.accountingtools.com/articles/what-is-accumulated-depreciation.html.

Bragg, S. (2019, March 29). Overview of depreciation: Depreciation accounting. Retrieved from https://www.accountingtools.com/articles/2017/5/15/overview-of-depreciation-depreciation-accounting.

Bragg, S. (2019, May 9). Accounting for intangible assets. Retrieved from https://www.accountingtools.com/articles/2017/5/17/intangible-assets-accounting-amortization.

Bragg, S. (2019, August 6). Budget definition. Retrieved from https://www.accountingtools.com/articles/what-is-a-budget.html.

Business Fraud: Culture Is the Culprit. (2017, November 14). Retrieved from https://business-ethics.com/2014/09/23/1840-business-fraud-culture-is-the-culprit/.

Calculating Cost of Goods Sold and Inventory Cost. (n.d.).
Retrieved from
https://www.dummies.com/business/accounting/calculating-cost-of-goods-sold-and-inventory-cost/.

California, S. of. (n.d.). Retrieved from
http://www.dof.ca.gov/budget/resources_for_departments/budget_analyst_guide/budgeting_accounting_relationship.html.

Careers in Accounting. (n.d.). Retrieved from
https://www.accountingedu.org/career-resources.html.

Cash Basis Accounting vs. Accrual Accounting: Bench
Accounting. (n.d.). Retrieved from
https://bench.co/blog/accounting/cash-vs-accrual-accounting/.

Cash Flow Statement. (2019, October 17). Retrieved from
https://en.wikipedia.org/wiki/Cash_flow_statement.

Cash Flow Statement: Explanation: AccountingCoach. (n.d.). Retrieved from https://www.accountingcoach.com/cash-flow-statement/explanation.

Cash Flow Statements, Explained: Bench Accounting. (n.d.). Retrieved from https://bench.co/blog/accounting/cash-flow-statements/.

Cash vs Accrual Accounting Explained. (n.d.). Retrieved from https://www.xero.com/us/resources/small-business-guides/accounting/cash-vs-accrual-accounting/.

Chatterjee, A. (n.d.). Top 13 accounting concepts – Explained! Retrieved from https://www.linkedin.com/pulse/top-13-accounting-concepts-explained-aroop-chatterjee.

Chen, J. (2019, October 8). Income statement definition. Retrieved from https://www.investopedia.com/terms/i/incomestatement.asp.

Cost Accounting - Budgeting Analysis. (n.d.). Retrieved from
https://www.tutorialspoint.com/accounting_basics/c
ost_accounting_budgeting_analysis.htm.

Cottonhead, Tessy, Sheoran, M., Wilson, Rajesh, Michelle, ...
Sanjana. (2019, September 24). Classification of
Accounts - Definition, Explanation and Examples.
Retrieved from
https://www.accountingformanagement.org/classifica
tion-of-accounts/.

Double-entry Bookkeeping System. (2019, October 15).
Retrieved from
https://en.wikipedia.org/wiki/Double-
entry_bookkeeping_system.

Doyle, A. (2019, September 14). Accounting careers: Job
options, titles, and descriptions. Retrieved from
https://www.thebalancecareers.com/accounting-job-
titles-2061488.

Edunote.info@gmail.com. (2019, June 16). 4 accounting
assumptions are explained. Retrieved from
https://iedunote.com/accounting-assumptions.

Elmblad, S. (2019, May 19). What is double entry accounting? Retrieved from https://www.thebalance.com/what-is-double-entry-accounting-1293675.

Estimated Useful Life and Depreciation of Assets. (2019, September 5). Retrieved from https://www.assetworks.com/useful-life-and-depreciation/.

Ethics and Fraud. (n.d.). Retrieved from https://www.uccs.edu/business/resources/ethics/focus-areas/fraud.

FAF, Financial Accounting Foundation. (n.d.). Retrieved from https://www.accountingfoundation.org/jsp/Foundation/Page/FAFBridgePage&cid=1176164538898.

FASB Accounting Standards Codification®. (n.d.). Retrieved from https://asc.fasb.org/.

FASB, Financial Accounting Standards Board. (n.d.). Retrieved from https://www.fasb.org/jsp/FASB/Page/LandingPage&cid=1175805317350.

Financial Accounting. (n.d.). Retrieved from
https://courses.lumenlearning.com/sac-finaccounting/chapter/inventory-methods-for-ending-inventory-and-cost-of-goods-sold/.

Fixed Asset Depreciation: RedBeam Articles. (n.d.). Retrieved from http://www.redbeam.com/fixed-asset-depreciation/.

Freedman, J. (2019, January 28). What is an "ethical issue" in financial accounting? Retrieved from https://smallbusiness.chron.com/ethical-issue-financial-accounting-57889.html.

GASB, Financial Accounting Standards Board. (n.d.). Retrieved from https://www.gasb.org/jsp/GASB/Page/GASBSectionPage&cid=1176168081485.

Generally Accepted Accounting Principles. (n.d.). Retrieved from https://www.cliffsnotes.com/study-guides/accounting/accounting-principles-i/principles-of-accounting/generally-accepted-accounting-principles.

Generally Accepted Accounting Principles (GAAP). (n.d.).
Retrieved from https://www.investor.gov/additional-resources/general-resources/glossary/generally-accepted-accounting-principles-gaap.

Generally Accepted Accounting Principles (United States).
(2019, October 9). Retrieved from
https://en.wikipedia.org/wiki/Generally_Accepted_Accounting_Principles_(United_States).

Grigg, B. A. (2019, October 12). Accounting principles:
Definitions and explanations. Retrieved from
https://www.fundera.com/blog/accounting-principles.

Hayes, A. (2019, October 8). Balance sheet definition.
Retrieved from
https://www.investopedia.com/terms/b/balancesheet.asp.

Hayes, A. (2019, October 17). How double entry works.
Retrieved from
https://www.investopedia.com/terms/d/double-entry.asp.

Hayes, A. (2019, October 16). Understanding cost of goods sold – COGS. Retrieved from https://www.investopedia.com/terms/c/cogs.asp.

Income statement. (2019, September 25). Retrieved from https://en.wikipedia.org/wiki/Income_statement.

Income Statement - Definition, Explanation and Examples. (n.d.). Retrieved from https://corporatefinanceinstitute.com/resources/knowledge/accounting/income-statement/.

Income Statement - Expense and Losses: AccountingCoach. (n.d.). Retrieved from https://www.accountingcoach.com/income-statement/explanation/3.

Income Statements: A Simple Guide: Bench Accounting. (n.d.). Retrieved from https://bench.co/blog/accounting/income-statement/.

Inventory and Cost of Goods Sold: Explanation:
AccountingCoach. (n.d.). Retrieved from
https://www.accountingcoach.com/inventory-and-
cost-of-goods-sold/explanation.

Investopedia. (2019, September 13). The difference between a
general ledger and a general journal. Retrieved from
https://www.investopedia.com/ask/answers/030915
/whats-difference-between-general-ledger-and-
general-journal.asp.

Kagan, J. (2019, October 8). Accountant. Retrieved from
https://www.investopedia.com/terms/a/accountant.a
sp.

Katre, H., ProfitBooks, & ProfitBooks. (2018, July 9). What is
depreciation - Types, formula & calculation methods
for small businesses accounting. Retrieved from
https://www.profitbooks.net/what-is-depreciation/.

Kenton, W. (2019, August 22). Trial balance. Retrieved from
https://www.investopedia.com/terms/t/trial_balance
.asp.

Kenton, W. (2019, October 11). Generally accepted accounting principles (GAAP). Retrieved from https://www.investopedia.com/terms/g/gaap.asp.

Kenton, W. (2019, September 11). Going Concern. Retrieved from https://www.investopedia.com/terms/g/goingconcer n.asp.

Kenton, W. (2019, August 28). Salvage value definition. Retrieved from https://www.investopedia.com/terms/s/salvagevalu e.asp.

King, S. (n.d.). Cash basis or accrual basis accounting: What's better? Retrieved from https://www.growthforce.com/blog/cash-basis-vs-accrual-basis-accounting-small-medium-businesses.

Ledger, General Ledger Role in Accounting Defined and Explained. (2019, September 11). Retrieved from https://www.business-case-analysis.com/ledger.html#journal242.

Lewis, M. R. (2019, March 29). How to calculate depreciation on fixed assets. Retrieved from https://www.wikihow.com/Calculate-Depreciation-on-Fixed-Assets.

Lewis, M. R. (2019, March 28). How to amortize assets. Retrieved from https://www.wikihow.com/Amortize-Assets.

Li, A. (2016, October 26). The effects of poor ethics in accounting. Retrieved from https://smallbusiness.chron.com/effects-poor-ethics-accounting-37750.html.

Luca Pacioli. (2019, October 21). Retrieved from https://en.wikipedia.org/wiki/Luca_Pacioli.

Manager. (n.d.). Retrieved from https://www.manager.io/guides/9119.

Managerial Accounting. (n.d.). Retrieved from https://courses.lumenlearning.com/sac-managacct/chapter/introduction-to-budgeting-and-budgeting-processes/.

Marendra, D., Fadiyah, S., & Kanya. (2019, March 26). Fixed assets & depreciation: Accounting principles: HashMicro. Retrieved from https://www.hashmicro.com/blog/fixed-assets-depreciation/.

Morah, C. (2019, September 18). How does accrual accounting differ from cash basis accounting? Retrieved from https://www.investopedia.com/ask/answers/09/accrual-accounting.asp.

Murphy, C. B. (2019, June 11). Understanding the cash flow statement. Retrieved from https://www.investopedia.com/investing/what-is-a-cash-flow-statement/.

Murray, J. (2019, January 14). How to amortize intangible assets under IRS section 197. Retrieved from https://www.thebalancesmb.com/amortizing-intangible-assets-under-irs-section-197-398307.

Murray, J. (2019, June 25). Calculating cost of goods sold - Step by step. Retrieved from https://www.thebalancesmb.com/how-to-calculate-cost-of-goods-sold-397501.

Non-GAAP Financial Measures. (2018). Retrieved from
https://www.sec.gov/divisions/corpfin/guidance/nongaapinterp.htm.

Northard, A. (2018, September 21). How to depreciate a fixed asset. Retrieved from
https://amynorthardcpa.com/how-to-depreciate-a-fixed-asset/.

Periodicity Assumption: Examples. (n.d.). Retrieved from
https://www.myaccountingcourse.com/accounting-principles/periodicity-assumption.

Putra, D. (2014, February 2). Basic accounting: Assumptions, principles, constraints. Retrieved from
http://accounting-financial-tax.com/2009/08/basic-accounting-assumptions-principles-constraints/.

QuickBooks. (2019, May 9). Cash vs. accrual accounting: What's best for your small business? Retrieved from
https://quickbooks.intuit.com/r/bookkeeping/cash-vs-accrual-accounting-whats-best-small-business/.

QuickBooks Canada Team. (2019, March 21). Classifying Assets on Balance Sheet. Retrieved from https://quickbooks.intuit.com/ca/resources/bookkeeping/classifying-assets-balance-sheet/.

Ramsey Solutions. (2019, October 3). What is an accountant and what do they do? Retrieved from https://www.daveramsey.com/blog/what-is-an-accountant.

Research Guides: Accounting: Ethics & fraud. (n.d.). Retrieved from https://guides.emich.edu/accounting/fraud.

Robert Half. (2018, July 26). In-demand accounting jobs - And how to land one. Retrieved from https://www.roberthalf.com/blog/job-market/in-demand-accounting-jobs-and-how-to-land-one.

Ruesink, M. (2018, March 26). 30 basic accounting terms, acronyms and abbreviations students should know. Retrieved from https://www.rasmussen.edu/degrees/business/blog/basic-accounting-terms-acronyms-and-abbreviations-students-should/.

Rules and Regulations for the Securities and Exchange
Commission and Major Securities Laws. (2017, May 12).
Retrieved from
https://www.sec.gov/about/laws/secrulesregs.htm.

Shpak, S. (2019, January 28). Five types of budgets in
managerial accounting. Retrieved from
https://smallbusiness.chron.com/five-types-budgets-
managerial-accounting-50928.html.

Staff, M. F. (2016, February 29). How to calculate the
amortization of intangible assets. Retrieved from
https://www.fool.com/knowledge-center/how-to-
calculate-the-amortization-of-intangible-as.aspx.

Standards & Guidance. (2019, September 27). Retrieved from
https://fasab.gov/accounting-standards/.

Statement of Cash Flows - How to Prepare Cash Flow
Statements. (n.d.). Retrieved from
https://corporatefinanceinstitute.com/resources/kno
wledge/accounting/statement-of-cash-flows/.

Stimpson, J., Padar, J., Hood, D., Mendlowitz, E., Cohn, M.,
Lee, D., … Root, D. (2019, October 21). By Jeff Stimpson.
Retrieved from https://www.accountingtoday.com/.

Summary: Budgeting. (n.d.). Retrieved from
https://www.accountingtools.com/summary-
budgeting.

The 10 Worst Corporate Accounting Scandals of All Time.
(2019, August 19). Retrieved from
https://www.accounting-degree.org/scandals/.

Top 5 Accounting Jobs. (n.d.). Retrieved from
https://www.topaccountingdegrees.org/top-5-
accounting-jobs/.

Trial Balance Period in Accounting Cycle Explained with
Examples. (2019, September 11). Retrieved from
https://www.business-case-analysis.com/trial-
balance.html.

Tuovila, A. (2019, September 28). Depreciation. Retrieved
from
https://www.investopedia.com/terms/d/depreciatio
n.asp.

Tuovila, A. (2019, August 28). Historical Cost Definition. Retrieved from https://www.investopedia.com/terms/h/historical-cost.asp.

Tuovila, A. (2019, May 22). Amortization of intangibles definition. Retrieved from https://www.investopedia.com/terms/a/amortization-of-intangibles.asp.

Tutorials, K. S. (n.d.). Accounting: The income statement and balance sheet. Retrieved from https://www.keynotesupport.com/accounting/accounting-balance-sheet-income-statement.shtml.

Types of Budgets - The Four Most Common Budgeting Methods. (n.d.). Retrieved from https://corporatefinanceinstitute.com/resources/knowledge/accounting/types-of-budgets-budgeting-methods/.

Understanding the Cash Flow Statement. (n.d.). Retrieved from https://www.abc-amega.com/Articles/Credit-Management/understanding-the-cash-flow-statement.

Vaidya, D., Vaidya, D., Vaidya, D., JPMorgan Equity Analyst, & JPMorgan Equity Analyst. (2019, July 22). Cash accounting vs accrual accounting: Top 9 differences. Retrieved from https://www.wallstreetmojo.com/cash-accounting-vs-accrual-accounting/.

Vaidya, D., Vaidya, D., & Vaidya, D. (2019, October 15). Amortization of intangible assets: Examples: Calculate. Retrieved from https://www.wallstreetmojo.com/amortization-of-intangible-assets/.

Ward, S. (2019, June 11). What exactly is a balance sheet? Retrieved from https://www.thebalancesmb.com/balance-sheet-definition-2946947.

What are the accounting principles, assumptions, and concepts?: AccountingCoach. (n.d.). Retrieved from https://www.accountingcoach.com/blog/accounting-principles-assumptions.

What Is A Balance Sheet: AccountingCoach. (n.d.). Retrieved
from https://www.accountingcoach.com/balance-
sheet/explanation.

What Is a Budget?: AccountingCoach. (n.d.). Retrieved from
https://www.accountingcoach.com/blog/what-is-a-
budget-2.

What Is a Trial Balance?: AccountingCoach. (n.d.). Retrieved
from https://www.accountingcoach.com/blog/what-
is-a-trial-balance.

What Is Accounting, Exactly?: Bench Accounting. (n.d.).
Retrieved from
https://bench.co/blog/accounting/what-is-
accounting/.

What Is Accounting? (2019, August 19). Retrieved from
https://www.accounting-degree.org/what-is-
accounting/.

What Is Budgeting?: AccountingCoach. (n.d.). Retrieved from
https://www.accountingcoach.com/blog/what-is-
budgeting.

What Is Periodicity in Accounting?: AccountingCoach. (n.d.).
Retrieved from
https://www.accountingcoach.com/blog/what-is-periodicity-in-accounting.

What Is the Difference between Inventory and the Cost of
Goods Sold?: AccountingCoach. (n.d.). Retrieved from
https://www.accountingcoach.com/blog/what-is-the-difference-between-inventory-and-the-cost-of-goods-sold.

What Is the Difference between the Cash Basis and the
Accrual Basis of Accounting?: AccountingCoach. (n.d.).
Retrieved from
https://www.accountingcoach.com/blog/cash-basis-accrual-basis-of-accounting.

What Is the Double-entry System?: AccountingCoach. (n.d.).
Retrieved from
https://www.accountingcoach.com/blog/what-is-the-double-entry-system.

What Is the Income Statement?: AccountingCoach. (n.d.).

 Retrieved from

 https://www.accountingcoach.com/blog/what-is-the-
income-statement.

Wood, M. (2019, August 3). Cash flow statement: What it is,

 example, and how to prepare one. Retrieved from

 https://www.fundera.com/blog/cash-flow-statement.

Writers, S. (2019, October 21). Career, degree and job

 information. Retrieved from

 https://www.accounting.com/.

Writers, S. (2019, July 22). The comprehensive guide to

 understanding GAAP. Retrieved from

 https://www.accounting.com/resources/gaap/.

ZipRecruiter. (n.d.). Retrieved from

 https://www.ziprecruiter.com/g/10-Most-Popular-
Types-of-Accounting-Jobs.